Managing Your Supply Chain Using Microsoft Navision

Scott Hamilton, Ph.D.

McGraw-Hill

New York   Chicago   San Francisco   Lisbon   London
Madrid   Mexico City   Milan   New Delhi   San Juan
Seoul   Singapore   Sydney   Toronto

The McGraw·Hill Companies

1 2 3 4 5 6 7 8 9 0 AGM/AGM 0 9 8 7 6 5

ISBN 0-07-143524-7

McGraw-Hill books are available at special quantity discounts to use as premiums and sales promotions, or for use in corporate training programs. For more information, please write to the Director of Special Sales, McGraw-Hill, Professional Publishing, 2 Penn Plaza, New York, NY 10121-2298. Or contact your local bookstore.

This book is printed on recycled, acid-free paper containing a minimum of 50% recycled de-inked fiber.

Library of Congress Cataloging-in-Publication Data

Hamilton, Scott, 1950-
    Managing your supply chain using Microsoft Navision / by Scott
Hamilton.
        p.   cm.
Includes index.
    ISBN 0-07-143524-7 (pbk. : alk. paper)
    1. Microsoft Navision. 2. Business logistics--Computer programs. I.
Title.
    HD38.5 .H35 2005
    658.7′0285′55—dc22
                                                            2003024117

Contents

Preface

The target audience for *Managing Your Supply Chain Using Microsoft Navision*[1] consists of those individuals involved with supply chain management in small to midsize manufacturing and/or distribution firms and divisions of large firms. These firms and divisions tend to have fewer than 500 employees. In particular, it is focused on those implementing or considering Microsoft Navision as their ERP system. My involvement with this target audience and Navision provided the impetus for writing this book. There were three motivating factors.

First, I would have liked a guide book when I was learning Navision. Something that explained how it all fit together to manage key business processes in manufacturing and distribution. Something like Cliff's Notes. Something that gave me a mental framework for putting together the details learned through hands-on experience and training courseware. I wanted to achieve an overall understanding of how to manage a business and its supply chain activities using Navision, and to achieve it as quickly as possible. Many within the target audience are faced with learning Navision and also want an accelerated learning process. Hence, the first motivating factor was to provide a guide to assist others in learning Navision.

The second motivating factor involved a desire to facilitate system implementation and ongoing usage. My efforts to train and consult with firms implementing an ERP system like Navision often involve explanations about effective system usage. These firms want to improve bottom-line results with improved coordination of supply chain activities. They want a vision of how an integrated ERP system could help achieve this. They want recommendations for improved business processes and how these could be modeled in the system. This typically requires an evaluation of fit between their requirements and the system's standardized functionality, and an identification of needed customizations. It often requires outside-of-the-box thinking and case studies from other environments to help stimulate discussion. In particular, these firms are looking for suggested changes that simplify and improve system usage. The suggested changes ideally incorporate the fundamental design factors within their ERP package. The last chapter summarizes these design factors,

---

[1] Navision is a registered trademark of Microsoft Corporation.

and explanations for effective system usage are embedded throughout this book along with case studies that highlight usage of standardized and customized functionality.

The third motivating factor involved a desire to assist those involved in Navision-related services and sales. They are charged with providing knowledgeable service across all interactions with their customers. This book reflects my experience in working alongside those serving the marketplace of small to midsize manufacturers and distributors. Our working relationship typically involved training and joint efforts at selling, consulting, and customer support. The book hopefully assists their efforts at serving the target audience.

The prior research for writing this book involved several different approaches to understanding Navision and the target audience. Starting from an end-user viewpoint, I went through the Navision training courses and hands-on exercises with other end users. My learning process was supplemented by going through the computer-aided instruction materials, reading the online documentation as part of my own hands-on experience, and talking with knowledgeable experts at resellers and Microsoft. These efforts represent the typical end-user learning process. Additional efforts were undertaken to supplement my learning process. These efforts included reading other materials (such as white papers and independent analyses of Navision), attending Navision presentations at various conferences, face-to-face meetings with current users to understand their system usage, and reviewing independently developed applications that extended Navision functionality. Most importantly, my learning process was supplemented by thousands of hands-on simulations to understand how the system really worked and how it solves the business problems of various manufacturing and distribution environments.

In terms of understanding the target audience, the prior research involved gaining an in-depth knowledge of various types of operations and the management team responsible for those operations. In this respect, the prior research built on my experiences as an MIS manager and production scheduler implementing various ERP systems in smaller firms, and face-to-face consulting engagements with over a thousand small to midsize manufacturing and distribution firms.[2] These engagements primarily focused on managing

---

[2] A synthesis of my consulting engagements has been published in two previous books. *Managing Information: How Information Systems Impact Organizational Strategy* (Irwin, 1993, with Gordon B. Davis) was one of the textbooks for the Certificate in Information Resource Management by the American Production and Inventory Control Society (APICS). *Maximizing Your ERP System: A Practical Guide for Managers* (McGraw-Hill, 2003) focuses on supply chain management in small to mid-size manufacturing firms.

supply chain activities and effective ERP system usage. Each engagement required interviews with the management team to gain an in-depth understanding of how they currently run (and want to run) their business, and facilitative discussions about ways to improve operations and ERP system effectiveness. These engagements covered the spectrum of variations in operations, company size, management background, levels of ERP expertise, terminology, geographies, and cultures across six continents. Each engagement required explanations that accounted for these variations in the target audience.

The more recent opportunities to consult with scores of firms implementing or considering Microsoft Navision have supplemented the foundation of prior research. Each engagement has broadened the ability to provide meaningful explanations about improving business processes and ERP system usage. Other venues have provided opportunities to meet the target audience and attempt to provide meaningful explanations through teaching and written materials. These other venues included teaching several hundred training seminars, software user group presentations, MBA classes, and classes for vocational-technical colleges and APICS certification. Attempts to provide written explanations have included my responses to hundreds of RFPs (requests for proposals) related to ERP systems, and scholarly articles based on field research and secondary research.[3]

One critical issue in writing this book involved the appropriate level of detail, especially given the objective of explaining how it all fits together to manage supply chain activities. The book attempts to provide a framework for organizing detailed information about how Navision works. This required a focus on key business processes and the key concerns of the target audience. The metric for these key processes and concerns is the frequency distribution of issues covered during face-to-face consulting engagements. The book employs more detailed explanations for these key processes and concerns. In addition, the book segments explanations into basic and advanced considerations, and provides scenarios illustrating different types of operations. This allows the

---

[3] Examples of relevant articles range from "Requirements of Smaller Manufacturers for Computer-Based Systems" (published in *APICS Quarterly*, Winter 1984) to "Trends Affecting Manufacturers and ERP" (published in *TechnologyEvaluation.com*, October 2003). More academic-oriented articles include an annual summary of the top MIS doctoral dissertations since 1973 (published in *MIS Quarterly*).

reader to focus on relevant material. It is hoped the explanations provide a balance between too much versus too little detail.[4]

A second critical issue in writing this book involved the evolving nature of software package functionality. The standardized functionality covered in this book reflects Release 3.7 (USA version), with partial foreknowledge of Release 4.0 functionality. It is the author's opinion that the fundamental design described here will not significantly change with the new release, thereby ensuring the book's applicability over the near-term horizon.

The book reflects my interpretation of how Microsoft Navision really works. Errors of omission and commission, and any misunderstandings, are hopefully minimized. Corrections and suggestions are welcome; send to ScottHamiltonPhD@aol.com. The intended goal is to provide a totality of understanding so readers can accelerate their learning process about managing their supply chain activities.

Each day of writing was started with the following prayer:

> Creator of all things, give me a sharp sense of understanding, a retentive memory, and the ability to grasp things correctly and fundamentally. Grant me the talent of being exact in my explanations, and the ability to express myself with thoroughness and charm. Point out the beginning, direct the progress, and help in the completion.

❄❄

Many people helped in completing this book, especially Catherine Dassopolous and Karen Schopp at McGraw-Hill, and Jan Degross and Judy Brown in editing and typesetting. Invaluable feedback was provided by numerous reviewers, and especially from Grant Barkman, Russ Bengtson, Terry Cook, Jerry Fors, Myles Halsband, Greg Hillenbrand, and Fred Holst. Their help deserves a special thank you.

---

[4] More detailed explanations are most effective in the context of company-specific issues and/or hands-on usage. The author conducts a separate seminar, with an optional exercise guide and database for hands-on exercises, which facilitates more detailed explanations. Contact the author for more information about this seminar.

Chapter 1

Introduction

Effective management of supply chain activities in manufacturing and distribution requires an integrated information system. This integrated information system is commonly referred to as an Enterprise Resource Planning (ERP) system. The term *ERP system* sometimes gets misconstrued as pertaining to just large companies or just a subset of applications. It is used here in its broadest sense—pertaining to companies large and small and to all integrated applications to run a manufacturing or distribution company.

Most small to midsize businesses opt for a software package as the foundation for an integrated ERP system. The package's standardized functionality provides the basic framework for supporting variations in business processes, with unique requirements covered by varying degrees of customization. Learning the standardized functionality represents a critical activity for system selection, implementation, and ongoing usage by individuals within these firms.

An individual's learning process usually builds on training courseware and hands-on experience. In many cases, these provide a detailed viewpoint expressed in software-specific terminology and a screen-by-screen walk-through approach. It makes an overall understanding difficult and requires time-consuming efforts to piece the details together into a mental framework. Most people can accelerate their learning process by starting with a mental framework of how the system fits together to run a business, expressed in generally accepted terminology. The mental framework—in combination with hands-on experience and training courseware—reduces the learning curve, and an overall understanding leads to more effective system usage.

This book addresses the need for an overall understanding of one ERP system: the Navision Edition from Microsoft Business Solutions, more simply referred to as Microsoft Navision.[1] It focuses on using Navision for managing supply chain activities in small to midsize manufacturing and distribution

---

[1] Navision is a registered trademark of Microsoft Corporation.

environments. Other integrated applications within Navision, such as accounting, human resources, customer relationship management, and service management (for repairing products), fall outside the scope of this book. The book's format enables readers to focus on information of particular interest:

- ◆ Focus on just distribution or manufacturing environments, or both
- ◆ Focus on single-site or multisite operations, or both
- ◆ Focus on key business processes to run a company
- ◆ Focus on standardized functionality, with case studies on customizations
- ◆ Focus on industry-specific case studies relevant to the reader
- ◆ Each chapter's Executive Summary provides a quick-read approach

The targeted reader includes those individuals implementing or considering Navision as their ERP system as well as those providing sales and implementation services. Firms involved with a system selection process may be considering Navision as a candidate package, and this book can help reduce selection risks, evaluate system fit and needed customizations, and provide a vision of an integrated system. For businesses involved in implementing and using Navision, the book can help accelerate the learning process, reduce implementation time and costs, reduce user resistance to change, and suggest changes to improve system usage. For firms providing Navision-related sales and services, this book can accelerate the employee learning process for providing knowledgeable customer service in sales, support, and professional assistance. Figure 1.1 summarizes these reasons for reading the book.

A Note about Design Factors Shaping System Usage

ERP system usage is shaped by several design factors related to the user interface, system functionality, and customization tools. For example, consistency and symmetry in the user interface and functionality make an ERP system easier to learn and use. The design factors shaping usage of Microsoft Navision are covered throughout this book and summarized in the concluding chapter. However, three design factors require up-front attention.

One design factor involves the terminology used to describe system usage. The functions, window titles, and field labels within Microsoft Navision have been used as much as possible to explain system functionality. However, alternative phrasing or generally accepted synonyms are sometimes used to clarify understanding. The Appendix contains illustrations of Microsoft Navision terminology and synonyms. It also defines the significance of several key

	Distribution or Manufacturing Firm	Solution Provider
Overall Goal	Improve firm performance through effective supply chain management systems	Improve firm performance through effective customer service
System Selection	Reduce selection risk Evaluate system fit and needed customizations Provide vision of an integrated system	Accelerate learning process Reduce new employee ramp-up time Improve solution-selling techniques Improve training and consulting efforts Improve customization capabilities
Implementation	Accelerate learning process Reduce implementation costs and time Reduce user resistance to change	
Ongoing Operation	Suggest changes to improve system usage	

(Left margin label: System Implementation Life Cycle)

Figure 1.1 Reasons for Reading the Book

terms—such as posting, journals, and ledger entries—that are essential for explaining system functionality.

A second key design factor involves the primary engine for coordinating supply chain activities. The primary engine is termed *planning calculations*. Using information about demands, this program calculates material and capacity requirements and generates suggested schedules for purchasing, manufacturing, and distribution. It communicates needed synchronization efforts via suggested action messages displayed on a worksheet. Planning calculations reflect the shop calendar of working days assigned to each location, customer, and vendor, as well as the shop calendar of working hours assigned to work centers.

A third design factor involves standardized functionality versus customizations. A focus on "out-of-the-box" or standardized functionality provides a baseline for learning how the system manages supply chain activities in different environments. But Navision is also highly customizable, with perhaps the best mix of ease-of-customization and power-of-customization available anywhere. Independent software vendors have also developed significant extensions. The general idea is that standard functionality meets 80 to 90 percent of a firm's requirements while customizations and independently developed extensions meet the remaining needs. Customizations can be used to tailor functionality to each firm's unique requirements, with the most frequently customized applications ranging from sales order processing, commissions, and sales analysis reports to document formats and production order travelers.

Key Business Processes and an Organizing Focus for the Book

Manufacturing and distribution companies share many similarities in their supply chain activities and ERP system requirements. In addition, many manufacturers operate as a distributor, selling purchased products or coordinating replenishment across their distribution network. Many distributors also operate as a manufacturer, performing light assembly. Some companies are in the midst of switching products from purchased to manufactured, or vice versa. Therefore, an overall understanding requires consideration of both environments. The starting point for an overall understanding consists of several key business processes built on a common database, with management reporting to support decision making across the organization.

The common database defines a firm's saleable products. For the purposes of this book, the common database can be viewed from the two perspectives of a distributor and a manufacturer.

Distribution Items and Purchased Material. Saleable products consist of purchased material in a distribution environment. These items are typically stocked in advance of sales orders but may be purchased to order.

Manufactured Items. A manufacturing environment also purchases material and then produces manufactured items either to stock or to order or both. The transformations from purchased material to manufactured item are minimally defined by bill of material information, with the processing steps and resource requirements optionally defined by routing information.

Six business processes can be identified for supply chain management in manufacturing and distribution environments. Three of these business processes revolve around sales orders, purchase orders, and production orders.

Sales Order Processing. The sales order process typically starts with sales order entry and finishes with shipment and customer invoices. It requires definition of customers, and involves related activities such as quotes and customer returns and the larger context of managing customer relationships.

Purchase Order Processing. The purchase order process typically starts with purchase order entry and finishes with receipts and vendor invoices. It requires definition of vendors, and involves related activities such as quotes and vendor returns and the larger context of managing vendor relationships. Coordination of purchasing activity focuses on suggested actions to replenish inventory or meet demand.

Production Order Processing. The production order process starts with creation of the production order and finishes with a completed product. Coordination of production activity focuses on production schedules by work center and suggested actions to replenish inventory or meet demand.

There are three additional business processes involving multisite operation, warehouse management, and sales and operations planning.

Multisite Operation. Some multisite operations involve transfer orders between locations. Starting with the creation of a transfer order, this involves shipping and receiving activities at the ship-from and ship-to locations. Multisite operations may also impact the other processes for sales orders, purchase orders, and production orders. For example, a sales order may identify line items with shipments from different locations with no requirement for a transfer order.

Warehouse Management. Warehouse management involves inbound and outbound shipments in support of the four above-mentioned business processes. For example, warehouse management involves receiving and put-away for purchase orders, and picking and shipment for sales orders. It also involves handling internal inventory movements and cycle counting. These activities taken as a group represent a key business process.

Sales and Operations Planning. One of the most critical business processes involves running the company from the top. This business process requires balancing sales demand against the ability of operations to supply product, and it is commonly termed the sales and operations planning (S&OP) process. It starts with the definition of all demands for the firm's products, and formulates S&OP game plans that drive supply chain activities to meet those demands. The nature of each game plan depends on the environment. An S&OP game plan can be expressed as master schedules for stocked items and/or finishing schedules for make-to-order items.

This simple mental framework provides an organizing focus for further explanation. The following chapters cover the common database information about purchased and manufactured items and the above-mentioned six business processes. Many firms conduct business as a single-site operation so that the chapter on multisite operations may not apply.

This format enables readers to focus on just distribution or manufacturing, and just single-site or multisite operations. For example, a single-site distributor can focus on the database for distribution items (Chapter 2) and their key business processes for planning, sales, purchasing, and inventory (Chapters 4, 5, 6, and 7). A single-site manufacturer can focus on the database for purchased material (Chapter 2) and manufactured items (Chapter 3), the basic business processes (Chapters 4 though 7), and the additional business processes involving production (Chapter 8). Chapter 9 covers the incremental information about multisite operations for both distribution and manufacturing environments, while Chapter 10 summarizes the design factors shaping system usage.

Each chapter provides a basic overview of critical information and variations in business processes supported by standardized functionality. Each chapter also includes an executive summary and case studies that highlight use of standardized and customized functionality.

The Baseline for Case Studies Used Throughout the Book

Case studies illustrate how standardized functionality applies to different types of environments, especially the flexibility to model variations in business processes. They also illustrate customizations that go beyond standardized functionality in solving business problems.[2]

The book's case studies reflect one distribution company, four manufacturing companies, and one catchall company. The catchall category allows coverage of case studies applicable to all five environments, and of case studies that represent different environments. These categories are shown in Figure 1.2 and the case study companies are briefly explained below.

Case A: All-and-Anything   The All-and-Anything company consists of several businesses that have been acquired. Each business operates autonomously and produces a unique set of products.

Case B: Batch Process   The Batch Process company manufactures two major product lines involving liquids and solids. It purchases materials and builds product to stock.

Case C: Consumer Products   The Consumer Products company manufactures electrical products and other products for the consumer marketplace. It purchases materials and builds product to stock.

---

[2] Customizations have been developed by Microsoft Navision partners for handling specialized requirements in numerous industries, ranging from manufacturers involved in animal production to distributors involved in food banks. A comprehensive listing of industry-specific customizations falls outside the scope of this book.

Companies

Chapter	Focus	A All-and-Anything	B Batch Process	C Consumer Products	D Distribution	E Equipment	F Fabrication
	Type of Products	Miscellaneous	Liquid & Solid	Electrical & Other	Industrial & Consumer	Industrial & Medical	Metal & Plastic
2	Purchased Material	1. Daily Usage Rates	2. Lot-Specific Costing	3. Rules-Based Pricing	4. Item Variants	5. Replacement Parts	6. Actual Costing
3	Manufactured Items	7. Virtual Manufacturing	9. Authorized Recipes	11. Printed Circuit Boards		13. Engineering vs. Production Bills	15. Cut-to-Size Material
		8. CAD Integration	10. By-Products	12. Item Variants in Bills		14. Common Bills	16. By-Products
4	Sales & Operations Planning	17. S&OP Simulations	18. Component Forecast	19. Kanban Coordination	20. S&OP by Job	22. Planning Bills	24. One-Time Product
					21. Statistical Forecasting	23. Manual MPS	
5	Sales Order Processing	25. Automotive Parts	27. Reserved Material	28. Mobile Order Entry		29. Product Configurator	
		26. Customer Merge				30. Smart Part Number	
6	Purchase Order Processing	31. Multistep Receiving	33. Conditional Releases	34. Vendor Schedules			35. Multiple Subcontractors
		32. Buyer Action Messages					
7	Warehouse Management	36. Stockroom Action Messages	37. Quality Management	38. ASNs and Bar-Coded Labels	39. Data Collection System	40. Shortage Reports	41. Warehouse Reports
8	Production Order Processing	42. Planner Action Messages	44. Regulated Mfg.			45. Customer-Supplied Parts	46. APS Integration
		43. Production Order Variances					
9	Multisite Operations	47. Centralized MPS		48. Multinational Food Products	49. Food Bank Distributor	50. Offshore Sales Company	

Figure 1.2 Summary of Case Studies

Case D: Distribution   The Distribution company represents a whole-saler carrying two major product lines—one for consumer products and another for industrial products—that are purchased and then sold from stock.

Case E: Equipment   The Equipment company manufactures industrial and medical products. Some standardized products are built to stock; other products are configured and built to order from stocked subassemblies.

Case F: Fabricated Products   The Fabricated Products company builds custom products to customer specification using metal and plastic raw materials.

Each chapter within the book includes case studies from these companies. Case studies that apply to all firms are grouped under Case A. Figure 1.2 summarizes the case studies by chapter and company.

Chapter 2

Distribution Items and Purchased Material

Information about material items provides the foundation for managing supply chain activities. Item information can be divided into company-wide and location-specific information. For example, company-wide information includes the item number, description, tracking policies, and pricing data, whereas location-specific information includes planning data for replenishing the location's inventory. Certain location-specific information must be defined whether a company operates as a single site or as multiple sites.

This chapter covers company-wide and location-specific information about purchased material items, including quality data, pricing data, costing data, planning data for suggested purchases, and warehouse stocking data. It also introduces other types of saleable items, such as item variants, non-stock items, kits of components, and resources of people or machine time.

The Item Master and Company-Wide Information

The item number represents the starting point for company-wide information about material items. Other considerations include the item description and item-related text. Company-wide information can be defined for quality, sales, and cost data. Some of the item's cost data, and additional data about planning and warehouse stocking, act as defaults for location-specific information.

Item Identification for Material

The item number provides a unique internal identifier for each material item, up to 20 characters in length. An item number can be manually or automatically assigned. Auto-numbering reflects a counter and optional prefix, and more than one auto-numbering scheme can be defined and used to assign item numbers.

In terms of item maintenance, a new item's information can be copied from an existing item and an existing item number can be changed or deleted prior to creation of ledger entries for the item. Changing (renaming) an existing item number will result in automatic updates to related information, such as changing the item number on a purchase order.

Several other considerations apply to item identification, including authorized units of measure, alternative identifiers for sales, purchasing, and warehousing purposes, and the significance of an item's revision level.

Authorized Units of Measure Each item can be assigned one or more authorized units of measure, or UM for short. However, one UM must be designated as the base UM for costing and inventory purposes. Examples of the user-defined UM codes include piece, box, kilogram, and liter. An item's base UM cannot be changed after ledger entries have been created. This single UM is sufficient for many environments.

Some environments require more than one authorized UM for an item. A different UM may be required for pricing, selling, or buying the item, defining vendor or customer item numbers, or for warehouse transactions. For example, an item's pricing may be expressed per piece and per box of 10. Each additional UM must be assigned to an item with an item-specific UM conversion factor expressed as a multiple or a fraction of the item's base UM. Entry of a fraction is translated to a decimal with precision up to five decimal places, so that an entry of 1/2000 translates to .0005.

Each authorized UM for an item can have physical dimensions, including length, width, height, volume, and weight. This optional information provides the basis for suggested warehouse put-aways that account for bin limitations of volume and weight. It could also be used for other purposes, such as calculating the total volume and weight for all lines on a sales order or purchase order.

An item's inventory can be stocked in multiple UM such as pallets and pieces. Planning and costing calculations understand the different inventory quantities in terms of the item's base UM. An item's inventory quantity in a given UM may need to be combined into a larger UM (or divided into a smaller UM) to satisfy a given requirement such as a sales order. The system can communicate the need for combining or dividing existing inventory quantities. For example, a pick document can communicate the need to break-bulk existing inventory for sales order shipment purposes.

Alternative Item Identifiers for Sales and Procurement Purposes An internal item number can be associated with other item identifiers for sales and procurement purposes. These are termed *item* *cross-references.* Each cross-reference number can be mapped to an internal item number and UM, and have a separate UM and description.

♦ *Sales Purpose.* The cross-reference number can be specified for a single customer to reflect a customer item number, or for all customers to reflect a catalog item. This mapping allows entry of the cross-reference number on a sales document rather than the internal item, with find capabilities based on the cross-reference number.

♦ *Procurement Purpose.* The cross-reference number can be specified for a single vendor to reflect a vendor item number, or for all vendors to reflect an industry standard. This mapping allows entry of the cross-reference number on a purchase document rather than the internal item, with find capabilities based on the cross-reference number.

Multiple cross-reference numbers can be defined for the same internal item number. For example, a customer may be changing their customer item numbers, or require different customer item numbers representing different units of measure.

Some industries have established a set of standardized or common item numbers, such as the Universal Product Code (UPC) or European Article Number (EAN) identifier. A common item number can be defined for each item, and subsequently used in exchanging information with customers and/or vendors in the supply chain. For example, it can identify items in inbound and outbound Biztalk documents.[1]

Alternative Item Identifier for Warehouse Management Purposes
Some warehousing environments require a different item number or UM for the purpose of inventory put-aways and picking. This requires a mapping between the internal item number (and base UM) and the warehouse item number and UM.

Significance of Revision Level
An item's revision level generally represents a level of documentation, and several terms (such as engineering change level) refer to the same concept. The significance of an item's revision level differs among firms, especially in terms of a change in form, fit, or function and the impact on interchangeability. One viewpoint treats revision levels as interchangeable, and revision level can be treated as an item attribute for

---

[1] A Biztalk document provides an electronic method of exchanging information with a customer or vendor, such as an order or quote. Chapter 10 summarizes the types of Biztalk documents, and they are also described for sales documents (Chapter 5) and purchasing documents (Chapter 6).

reference purposes. A second viewpoint considers revision level as part of the item's unique identifier (such as embedding it in the item number) so that revision levels are not interchangeable.

Other Considerations About Material Items

So far the explanation of material items has focused on item identification. Additional considerations include the item description, item-related text, and item attributes.

Item Description   The item description represents one of the key attributes of an item. It is used for finding an item and for communicating to internal and external personnel. The basic approach for defining an item's description—a single, 30-character field—is sufficient for many environments, whereas other situations require more detailed description information.

- ◆ *Description Line 1.* A description field consists of 30 characters.
- ◆ *Description Line 2.* A second description field consists of 30 characters.
- ◆ *Search Description.* A separate search description field of 50 characters defaults to the item description line 1, and can be overridden.
- ◆ *Language-Specific Description.* Two description lines can be defined for each alternative language code
- ◆ *Extended Text.* Extended text consists of multiple lines of free-form text, as described in the next section.

Item-Related Text   Item-related text in Navision can be specified in two ways: as comments or as extended text.

- ◆ *Comments.* Item comments are generally used for internal purposes, and can be defined with multiple lines of free-form text. Each line may be assigned a user-defined code to sort and filter comments, such as filtering comments related to engineering or quality specifications.
- ◆ *Extended Text.* Extended text for an item is generally used for external purposes, and can be defined with multiple lines of free-form text. You can selectively designate whether the extended text will appear on various types of sales and purchasing documents, such as quotes, orders, blanket orders, return orders, invoices, and credit memos. Effectivity dates and a language code can be assigned to an extended text. The extended text can be automatically added to line items on sales and purchase documents (based on an item policy), or you can manually

request insertion of extended text on a line item. The extended text description can be overridden on the document.

Item Attributes and Analytic Dimensions   Item attributes help differentiate items and serve multiple purposes. For example, they can be used to find items, to filter information displayed on a screen, and as parameters that filter information displayed on reports. Examples of item attributes include the duty class, country of origin, and picture number.

An analytical dimension represents a unique type of item attribute for the purpose of business analytics or business intelligence. The term does not represent a physical dimension of the item. Rather, it supports multidimensional reporting capabilities such as sales analysis by product group and customer group. Dimensions are also assigned to other entities, such as customers, salespeople, and sales campaigns, to support multidimensional reporting.

Quality Data

Quality management for material items involves many facets, including vendor approval and policies about lot and serial tracking. These represent company-wide policies for supporting quality management concerns.

Item Tracking Policies for Lot- and Serial-Traced Material

Quality management policies identify which items require enforcement of lot tracking, serial tracking, and expiration tracking. They are collectively termed *item tracking* policies.

- ◆ *Lot Tracking.* Lot tracking can be enforced across all transaction types or selectively enforced by transaction type. The transaction types include purchase order receipts and returns, sales order shipments and returns, inventory adjustments, transfers, warehouse transactions, and production order completions. For example, some items only require lot assignment upon sales order shipment. You can optionally enforce recording of quality metrics for each lot number.
- ◆ *Serial Tracking.* Serial tracking can be similarly enforced across all transaction types or selectively enforced by transaction type such as serialization upon shipment. You can optionally enforce recording of quality metrics for each serial number.
- ◆ *Expiration Tracking and Warranty Date.* An expiration date can be manually assigned to incoming material and enforced so that the material cannot be issued after the expiration date. At time of shipment, a warranty date can also be assigned manually or automatically based on

a date formula such as one year or 18 months. The policies concerning expiration tracking and warranty dates can apply to items that are not lot or serial traced.

These policies ensure that the system prevents transaction posting until the item tracking information has been recorded. The posted transactions are retained in an audit trail termed *item tracking entries*. The system also prevents a change in item tracking policies after item ledger entries exist. For example, a lot-traced item cannot have its policies changed to non-tracked. A set of item tracking policies is identified with a user-defined *item tracking code*, and the code is subsequently assigned to relevant items.

Approved Vendors   Quality management typically assists in identifying an item's approved vendors, or conversely a vendor's approved items. Approved vendors are identified in terms of cross-reference information about the vendor item. The approved vendors (and cross-reference information) can be viewed and selected as part of purchase order processing.

Sales Data for Items

The company-wide information for sales purposes includes the definition of an item's price and applicable discounts. Some firms focus on item pricing without discounts, while others focus on discounts off a list price and/or discounts related to total order value. Sales-related data also includes the identification of substitute items and policies about reservations and capable-to-promise logic.

Sales Price Data   Standardized item pricing can be defined using three different approaches: a single base price, a sales price worksheet, and a campaign price worksheet. Other approaches to defining an item's price include a sales quote and blanket order, as explained in Chapter 5.

* *Base Price and Default Sales UM.* Each item can have a single base price expressed in its base UM. The item's base price can be entered directly or calculated in terms of the item's cost and profit percentage. The item's base price provides a simple approach to automatic pricing on sales orders. It acts as the default price on a sales order when other sources of information do not exist, such as a sales price worksheet.

    In some cases, an item is priced and sold in different units of measure than its base UM. These must be defined as authorized UM for the item, and one of these units of measure can be designated as the default sales UM. This means it acts as a default on sales orders; it can

Factor		Sales Price Worksheet	Sales Line Discount Worksheet	Campaign	
				Sales Price	Sales Line Discount
Item	Item and UM	X	X	X	X
	Group of Items		X Item Discount Group		X Item Discount Group
Bill to Customer	Customer		X		
	Group of Customers	X Customer Price Group	X Customer Discount Group		
	All Customers	X	X	X	X
Parameters	Date Effectivity	X	X	Tied to Campaign Effectivity Dates	Tied to Campaign Effectivity Dates
	Quantity Breakpoints	X	X	X	X
	Currency Code	X	X	X	X
	Policies	Price Includes Tax Allow Line Discount Allow Invoice Discounts		Price Includes Tax Allow Line Discounts Allow Invoice Discounts	
	Related Policies		Customer Policy: Allow Line Discount		Customer Policy: Allow Line Discount

Figure 2.1   Sales Prices and Line Discounts

be optionally overridden on the sales order with another one of the item's UM.

◆ *Sales Price Worksheet.* A sales price worksheet provides a more comprehensive approach to item pricing, and supports automatic pricing during sales document entry. Entries in the sales price worksheet typically represent a predefined price book or negotiated prices with specific customers. Item pricing often reflects one or more factors, as shown in Figure 2.1 and illustrated below.

— Pricing by item and unit of measure, such as different prices per item and per pallet.

— Pricing for a single customer, all customers, or a group of customers. The customer price groups, for example, could represent wholesalers and retailers.

— Pricing by currency code, such as separate pricing for foreign sales.

— Pricing with date effectivities, for supporting annual price updates or seasonal price promotions. Price assignment reflects the order date on a sales document.

A simple pricing scheme that represents this year's list price, for example, would require one worksheet entry for each saleable item, with date effectivities for each entry. A second set of worksheet entries would be required for defining next year's list price. Each worksheet entry also indicates policy information, such as whether the price includes tax.

The system automatically assigns an item's price during sales document entry, using the lowest price of applicable worksheet entries. The user can view available prices, such as quantity breakpoints or future pricing to guide customer decisions, but cannot select a price that does not match criteria such as the order quantity and date.

◆ *Campaign Price Worksheet.* A campaign serves several purposes with respect to customer interactions. It also provides a named price book approach to defining sales prices and line discounts. Each campaign has a unique identifier and date effectivities, and must be activated (and deactivated) to allow usage. A campaign has two worksheets, one for sales prices and one for line discounts.

Each entry in the campaign price worksheet defines an item and price, and other factors as shown in Figure 2.1. Campaign price worksheet entries act just like sales price worksheet entries. For example, the system automatically assigns the lowest price of applicable worksheet entries within either worksheet, and the user can view applicable entries from either worksheet. The campaign identifier can be entered on the sales order header, but it does not affect the use of price worksheets.

Sales Line Discounts   Once an item's price has been identified on a sales document, discounts can be optionally applied to the line item and/or the order total value. The discount related to total order value is termed an *invoice discount*. Invoice discounts are defined by customer and further explained in Chapter 5.

A line item discount can be manually or automatically assigned to a sales order line item. A manually entered discount can be expressed as a percentage or an amount (per the specified sales UM). Automatic assignment reflects a discount percentage defined in a sales line discount worksheet or a campaign worksheet.

◆ *Sales Line Discount Worksheet.* The definition and use of a sales line discount worksheet are very similar to a price worksheet. Line discounts often reflect one or more factors, as shown in Figure 2.1 and illustrated below.

— Discounts for a single customer, all customers, or a group of customers. The customer discount groups, for example, could be large and small accounts.

— Discounts for a single item or group of items. The item discount groups, for example, could represent different product lines.

A simple discounting scheme involving a discount percent by customer group, for example, would require one worksheet entry for each customer group. A policy defined for sales price worksheet entries determines whether line discounts can be applied. For example, line discounts may be excluded for price worksheet entries that define special pricing. A customer policy also determines whether line discounts apply to the customer.

- *Campaign Line Discount Worksheet.* As described above, a campaign has a unique identifier and date effectivities, and must be activated (and deactivated) to allow usage. A campaign has one worksheet for sales prices and another one for line discounts. Each entry in the campaign line discount worksheet defines a discount percentage for an item or item discount group, and other factors as shown in Figure 2.1. The campaign line discount worksheet entries act just like other worksheet entries. For example, the user can view and select applicable worksheet entries from either worksheet.

Substitute Items for Sales Purposes

A substitute item typically represents an alternative product that can be suggested during sales order entry when the desired item is unavailable. One or more substitute items can be defined for a product, with information about interchangeability and textual explanation about its conditions for usability. When the substitute item is flagged as interchangeable, it gets assigned the equivalent substitute item information. The sales order window flags a line item when the product has substitutes; this notifies users to view information and availability about the substitute item(s). The user's selection of a substitute item will update information on the sales order line item, and the system automatically retains the originally entered item.

Supporting Reservations and Capable-to-Promise

An item's *reservation policy* determines whether its inventory can be reserved for a sales order. The policies are never, optional, and always. The *optional reserve policy* allows manual or automatic reservations of the item's inventory. The *always reserve policy* means the item's inventory gets reserved automatically. The optional policy is most commonly used. A similar reservation policy can be defined for a customer, and this acts as a default on sales orders to the customer. Reservations represent hard allocations of inventory to sales orders. The use of reservations should be balanced against the loss of flexibility (such as using the inventory for another sales order) and the associated complexity of reserving (and unreserving) material.

One policy (termed the *critical policy*) determines whether an item can be checked for available-to-promise and/or capable-to-promise during sales order entry. This policy is normally assigned to just saleable end-items and/or to make-to-order components of a manufactured item.

Costing Data for Purchased Material

Item costs provide the basis for valuing inventory transactions. An item's costs can be based on a standard costing or actual costing approach, and each item can be assigned its own costing method. This explanation of costing data focuses on standard costing since it since it is a common and easily understood method of cost accounting.

Standard Cost for a Purchased Item   The standard cost for a purchased item consists of a direct material cost and an optional overhead cost. An item's direct material cost provides the basis for calculating purchase price variances, while the combined costs of material and overhead are used for valuing inventory transactions. Entry of an item's standard cost data reflects the combined costs. A separate entry identifies the material-related overhead factor, expressed as an amount or percentage or both. Hence, subtracting overhead cost from the combined costs derives an item's direct material cost.

Standard costs for purchased material represent company-wide information for cost roll-up purposes. The system maintains one set of standard cost data with one cost per item. Additional sets of costing data can be defined and maintained on a costing worksheet. On a periodic basis, the information in a costing worksheet can be used to update the items' standard costs. Note that standard costs can be manually maintained for an item's authorized locations, as described in the next section concerning location-specific information.

The system can automatically maintain additional sets of data for an item's average cost and last purchase cost, termed the last direct cost. The last direct cost and average cost are automatically updated based on posting of vendor invoices.

Actual Costing for a Purchased Item   An actual costing method is typically required because of widely varying purchase costs for an item. Typical examples include precious metals or commodities. Actual costing can be handled by several different methods, where the method determines the basis for valuing inventory. The actual costing method for an item can be based on average cost, last-in, first-out (LIFO), first-in, first-out (FIFO), and a serial-number specific cost. Actual costs get updated after posting a vendor's invoice. The actual costing methods handle situations where some inventory must be valued at zero cost, such as customer-supplied material or a customer return.

Actual costing methods involve increased system complexity in any ERP system, especially when the material is used or sold prior to posting the vendor's invoice. Further explanation of actual costing methods falls outside the scope of this book, although two case studies (see Cases #2 and #6) illustrate actual costing.

G/L Account Number Assignment for an Item An item's general ledger (G/L) account numbers are based on several user-defined posting groups assigned to the item. For example, the item's General Product Posting Group (in conjunction with a General Business Posting Group assigned to a customer or vendor) identifies the sales revenue and cost of sales account numbers, and the purchase and purchase price variance account numbers. The item's Inventory Posting Group identifies the location-specific balance sheet account for inventory.

Purchase Price Data Various forms of vendor agreements define pricing and/or discounts for purchased material. For example, a vendor agreement often specifies company-wide item prices and discount percentages. A vendor agreement may also be expressed as a purchase quote or blanket purchase order. Chapter 6 provides further explanation of vendor agreements.

The Item Master and Location-Specific Information

Companies can operate with one or more locations. The majority of smaller firms involve single-site operations. The terms location, site, warehouse, and plant are considered synonyms and will be used interchangeably. A location typically represents a physical site for inventory purposes such as a distribution center or manufacturing plant. It can also represent a logical site, such as a location for reserved material or material placed on hold. The location window defines information about a location, such as address information and several warehouse management policies that will be covered in Chapter 7. Each location can have one or more bins, and the combination of location and bin uniquely identifies the whereabouts of an item's inventory.[2]

Several aspects of item master information are location specific, such as planning data concerning inventory replenishment at a location. The loca-

---

[2] Information about a location includes a warehouse management policy that determines whether bins can be defined for the location. Almost all manufacturing and distribution firms require bins for tracking inventory whereabouts, whereas some firms using Microsoft Navision have simpler environments that do not require bins. Navision provides a simpler solution for these firms, where a suggested shelf can be identified for each item, but this only provides reference information about where the item's inventory might be found.

In addition to the solution that avoids use of bins, a simpler solution for single-site operations avoids the use of locations. This is termed the null location approach. However, a null location cannot have bins, so that most single-site companies involved in manufacturing and distribution define one location code to enable use of bins.

tion-specific information can only be maintained for an item's authorized locations, and an item can have one or more authorized locations.[3]

The combination of item number and authorized location is termed a *stockkeeping unit* (or SKU for short), and each SKU defines location-specific information. For example, a purchased item stocked in two locations (and therefore identified by two SKU numbers) might have different vendors and min-max replenishment logic for each location. Alternatively, one location may purchase the material while the second location gets replenished from the first via transfer orders.

Defining an authorized location for an item involves a process termed *create stockkeeping unit* (or the *create SKU process* for short). The creation of an item's SKUs involves an extra step after defining the item. Using the create SKU process, the item's SKUs can be created for all locations or for designated locations. The location-specific information initially reflects default values defined for the item. After creating SKUs, the location-specific information can be replaced at any time with new default values from the item (using the create SKU process with the option to just replace SKU information).

A comparison of an item's company-wide information and location-specific information is shown in Figure 2.2. The location-specific information consists of planning, cost, and warehouse stocking data.

Planning Data for Suggested Purchases

Creation of a purchase order for material typically stems from planning calculations that suggest a new purchase. It can also reflect manual planning or a system-generated suggestion related to a sales order for a drop-shipment or special order. The planning calculations suggest a new purchase based on SKU planning data about the item's primary source of supply, lead-time, and reordering policy, as described below. The suggested purchases can be organized by buyer responsibility.

Buyer Responsibility   The concept of buyer responsibility provides an organizing focus for communicating the need to synchronize supplies with demands. By assigning buyer responsibility to items and purchase orders, sug-

---

[3] The concept of an authorized location only affects the ability to have location-specific information such as planning data. It does not affect the ability to use any location for stocking an item's inventory, taking sales orders for shipment from a location, or creating purchase orders for delivery to a location.

			Item	Stockkeeping Unit (SKU)
		Identifier	Item Number	Item Number + Location
Company-Wide Information	Basic Data	Description		
		Base UM + Other UM		
		Cross-Reference Information		
		Approved Vendors		
		Lot/Serial Tracking Policies	Defined as Company-Wide Information	
		Extended Text		
	Sales	Sales Price Data		
		Substitute Items		
	Cost	Purchase Price Agreements		
		General Product Posting Group		
		Costing Method		
		Overhead Factors		
		Standard Cost Calculations		
Location-Specific	Planning Data	Replenishment System Policy		
		Default Vendor		
		Item Lead-Time	Define by Item (acts as the default value for each SKU)	Define by SKU (with initial default value from item)
		Reordering Policy		
		Order Modifiers		
	Cost	Standard Cost		
		Last Direct Cost		
		Inventory Posting Group		
		Comments	Define by Item	Define by SKU

Figure 2.2   Information for Items vs. Stockkeeping Units

gested action messages can be directed to the responsible buyer. Two approaches to indicate buyer responsibility are illustrated below.

- *General Product Posting Group Field.* Using this field to indicate buyer responsibility, suggested actions about new purchases and existing purchase order line items can be directed to the buyer. It can be optionally overridden on a line item to indicate a change in buyer responsibility. It also provides a means to track and analyze purchase price variances by buyer through general ledger entries.
- *Product Group Code Field.* Using this field to indicate buyer responsibility achieves the same results as above, but does not support the purchase variances by buyer.

Chapter 6 provides further explanation of suggested action messages about purchase orders.

Primary Source of Supply   A purchased SKU's primary source of supply is identified by a make/buy code (termed the *replenishment system*) and a default vendor. Additional company-wide information can be defined about an item's approved vendors, with information about the vendor item numbers and lead-times. The suggested action message for a new purchase initially identifies the SKU's default vendor, but the approved vendors can be viewed and selected prior to taking further action.

Lead-Time   Purchasing lead-time represents the typical notification period to place and receive a purchase order, identified as the start date and planned receipt date for a suggested purchase. Purchasing lead-time can be specified in three places—for the vendor item, the vendor, and/or the item—which the system uses in descending order of preference. For example, suggestions for a new purchase initially reflect the vendor item's lead-time (if specified) for the default vendor. Selection of a different approved vendor (and vendor item) can result in a different purchasing lead-time. The item lead-time provides a simple model of purchasing lead-time, whereas the vendor or vendor item lead-time allows differentiation of lead-time based on the source.

Purchasing Lead-Time and Capable-to-Promise Logic

Capable-to-promise (CTP) logic provides one approach to making sales order delivery promises for an out-of-stock item. CTP logic calculates a purchased item's earliest ship date based on the item's purchasing lead-time, where this lead-time depends on whether it has been defined for the vendor item, the vendor, or the item as described above.

Reordering Policy   A reordering policy and related planning data represent a model of the buyer's decision-making logic concerning purchase quantity and reorder cycle. The purchase quantity often reflects considerations of order modifiers. Order modifiers include a quantity minimum or multiple, or a maximum quantity that may result in multiple purchase orders for a fixed quantity to cover requirements. Reordering policies can be categorized by their underlying logic, such as time-phased order point logic, MRP logic, order-driven, and manual.

There are five reordering policies, as shown in Figure 2.3 and summarized below. Each reordering policy can be characterized by its primary planning parameters, order modifiers, and inventory plan approach.

	Reordering Policy	Planning Parameters		
	Significance and Synonym	Primary	Modifiers	Inventory Plan
TIME-PHASED ORDER POINT	Fixed Reorder Quantity Suggested order for reorder quantity (aka reorder point)	Reorder Quantity Reorder Point	Minimum Order Multiple Maximum	Safety Stock Safety Lead-Time
TIME-PHASED ORDER POINT	Maximum Quantity Suggested order achieves maximum inventory quantity (aka min-max)	Maximum Inventory Reorder Point	Minimum Order Multiple Maximum	Safety Stock Safety Lead-Time
MRP LOGIC	Lot for Lot Suggested order covers multiple demands within reorder cycle (aka period lot size)	Reorder Cycle Include Inventory	Minimum Order Multiple Maximum	Safety Stock Safety Lead-Time
ORDER DRIVEN	Order Suggested order covers one demand			Safety Lead-Time
MANUAL	Null No suggested orders (aka manual planning)			

Figure 2.3 Reordering Policies

- *Fixed Reorder Quantity (also known as Reorder Point).* When an item's projected inventory falls below its *reorder point*, the system suggests a *reorder quantity* subject to order modifiers and forward scheduled from the date.

- *Maximum Quantity (also known as Min-Max or Order-Up-To).* When an item's projected inventory falls below its *reorder point*, the system suggests an order quantity that achieves the item's *maximum quantity* subject to order modifiers and forward scheduled from the date.

- *Lot-for-Lot (also known as Period Lot Size).* When an item's projected inventory reaches zero (or its safety stock quantity), the system suggests an order quantity that covers demands over the *reorder cycle*, subject to order modifiers. A reorder cycle reflects the frequency of replenishment. The system backward schedules the proposed order from the due date.

  The lot-for-lot policy provides an option for including or excluding inventory in MRP logic; MRP logic still considers scheduled receipts regardless of the choice. As a general guideline, inventory should always be considered unless there are compelling reasons for ignoring existing stock.

- *Order.* The system suggests an order quantity that covers each individual demand, with the proposed order backward scheduled from the due date. It ignores order modifiers, but does consider safety lead-time.

◆ *Manual.* The system does not suggest orders, but does calculate projected inventory based on demands and supplies.

Several suggestions apply to these replenishment methods. For stocked material in a distribution environment, the simplest replenishment methods are based on time-phased order point or MRP logic. The time-phased order point methods are easy to understand and administer, especially with reasonably stable and independent demands. They do not require a sales forecast, but do recognize future demands in suggestions for future orders. They utilize order modifiers to model buyers' decision-making logic. However, changing demand patterns require updates to the planning parameters. An MRP-based method generally requires visibility of projected demand, expressed as future sales orders, sales forecast, and/or transfer order requirements. Using the frequency of replenishment defined by reorder cycle, the system automatically adjusts suggested order quantities to cover increasing or decreasing demands. Order modifiers can produce a dampening effect.

An inventory plan for stocked material can be expressed in several different ways. With order point methods, suggested order quantities can represent an implicit inventory plan when inflated by order modifiers, or when the reorder quantity exceeds typical demand over the reorder cycle. The order modifiers and reorder cycle provide a similar implicit inventory plan for MRP logic. An explicit inventory plan can be identified as an item's safety stock quantity or safety lead-time. The safety lead-time represents a buffer against delayed receipts, and also represents a demand-sensitive inventory plan.

Costing Data for Purchased Material

The item's standard costs and overhead factors are used in cost roll-up calculations for a standard cost item. Overhead factors represent company-wide information. The item's standard cost and last direct cost act as a default for location-specific costs, but the values can be manually overridden for an SKU. Each item's inventory posting group defines location-specific information for G/L account numbers such as inventory. Average costs are automatically calculated for either items or SKUs according to an inventory setup policy.

Warehouse Stocking Data

Within each authorized location for an item, the SKU can have one or more authorized bins (termed fixed bins) and one default bin. The default bin provides a basic approach for suggesting where to put incoming inventory and where to find inventory for picking purposes. The default bin can be manually or automatically designated. Manual designation of the default bin indicates a static assignment. To support dynamic assignment, the system can automatically update the default bin based on the last put-away transaction. An item may be placed in any bin.

Each SKU can have a counting frequency for cycle counting purposes, such as six times per year. The counting frequency typically reflects an ABC analysis of item usage and value, but it can be based on other factors.

Use of Location Information for a Single-Site Company

A majority of smaller companies operate as a single location. Therefore only one location (and its bins) needs to be defined, and each item will have a single SKU. Using default values throughout the system minimizes the impact of identifying the location in transactions, as described below.

- *Item Information.* The item information provides default values for the SKU cost, planning, and warehouse stocking data. Performing the create SKU function can automatically update the SKU data with new default values.
- *Customer Information.* Specify the single location as the preferred ship-from location for each customer (and customer ship-to address) so that it acts as a default on all sales documents.
- *Vendor Information.* Specify the single location as the preferred ship-to location for each vendor (and vendor ship-from address) so that it acts as a default on all purchase documents.
- *Forecasts.* Forecasts must be specified for the single location, and planning calculations will suggest replenishment for the location.

A company with a single physical location often defines additional logical locations, such as a location for material placed on hold or reserved for sales orders.

Other Types of Items

Purchased material represents one type of item with information defined and maintained in the item master. There are other types of items, such as item variants, non-stock items, kit items, resources, and service items.

Item Variants

Some purchased items have variations that can be uniquely identified by item number and a variant code. Typical examples involve variations in color and size, such as baseball hats or colored pens. An item with two variations of color (red and blue) and size (small and large) would require four variant codes (small red, small blue, large red, large blue). Creation of item variants involves two steps after defining the item. The authorized variant codes are first defined for the item, and a separate function generates the combinations of items and variant codes. These combinations are also termed stockkeeping units. Further explanation focuses on items and coverage of item variants will be limited to special cases. Cases #4 (in this chapter) and #12 (in Chapter 3) provide illustrations of item variants.

Variant codes often provide the starting point for customizations since they differentiate supplies, demands, costs, and prices for an item. For example, customizations have extended item variant functionality to handle significant revision levels and identification of custom configurations.

Non-Stock Items

A non-stock item typically represents a special order item. A non-stock item is similar to a material item with its own item master record and inventory tracking. However, a non-stock item has a slightly different approach to its creation and item numbering. A separate screen is used to define a non-stock item, where a vendor, vendor item number, and manufacturer's code must be specified. An additional function creates the non-stock item in the item master, using the vendor item number (or the vendor item plus a manufacturer's code) as the item number. It is flagged as a non-stock item in the item master to facilitate filter and finder capabilities, but acts like a material item in all other respects. A non-stock item can have costing and pricing data, multiple approved vendors and price quotes, extended text, a bill of material, and routing. It is included in standard cost calculations and MRP calculations. The planning data for a non-stock item can be defined, but it initially defaults to manual planning.

Kit Items

A kit item (termed a *BOM item*) typically represents a product requiring light assembly of its components prior to shipment. Two common scenarios involve selling a kit item as a single item or a set of component items. A kit item is defined on the item master just like other material items but it requires additional information about its components. Termed an *assembly list*, the kit's components can be material items, resource items, or other kit items. The system automatically flags a kit item on the item master after its assembly list has been created. Further explanation of kit items falls outside the scope of this book.

Resource Items

A resource represents an internal work center, such as a manufacturing cell, a group of similar machines, or a group of people with similar skills. A resource item provides one approach for selling time (rather than material), such as engineering services time or manufacturing time to perform a value-added operation on customer-supplied material. A resource item can be identified on a sales document line, and subsequently shipped and invoiced without requiring an inventory balance (unlike material items). Definition of a resource item includes costing and pricing information. The ability to sell time represents one purpose of a resource item. A second purpose involves resource components to represent routing operations for a kit item. Further explanation of resources falls outside the scope of this book.

Service Items

A service item represents a shipped product that requires service management. It can be mapped to an internal item number and serial number. A service item can be manually added, or automatically added based on a sales order shipment of an internal item number. The material and resource requirements to repair a service item are defined for a service order, and the item's assembly list can be used to initially define component requirements. Service items and their related service orders fall outside the scope of this book.

Case Studies

Case #1: Daily Usage Rates   The All-and-Anything company extended the types of reordering policies to include replenishment methods based on daily usage rates. Two daily usage rates were automatically calculated for each item, one based on historical usage and another on projected usage. The new reordering policies employed an item's designated daily usage rate so that order point logic automatically calculated the item's reorder point and quantity, while MRP logic calculated the item's safety stock.[4] Additional purposes are served by daily usages rate, such as Kanban coordination of production activities as described in Case # 21 (Chapter 4).

---

[4] See *Maximizing Your ERP System* for further explanation of daily usage rates, including fixed versus variable usage rates (p. 112), how to use daily usage rates in replenishment methods (pp. 117–120), and Kanban coordination of production activities (pp. 282–284).

Case #2: Lot-Specific Costing   The Batch Process company produced a food product line—bottles of mustard—from purchased lots of different types of mustard seeds. The purchased seeds required lot tracking, with quality and taste attributes associated with each lot. The manufacturing process involved mixing batches of mustard seeds into a paste that was packaged in various bottle types with different labels and cases. The lots of purchased material could be tracked to a daily production run, with the lot number assigned to each case and bottle representing the daily production run. This date serves as the basis for indicating shelf life. With a minor customization, the system supported a lot-specific costing method for the purchased lots of raw material.

Case #3: Rules-Based Pricing in Consumer Products   T h e Consumer Products company extended the sales price worksheet and invoice discount capabilities to include rules for each entry. Examples of rules-based pricing included "buy 10 and get one free" and "buy $1000 and get a free display case," where the rule automatically created an additional line item on the sales order. Additional price worksheet considerations included pricing based on delivery date (to promote early delivery of seasonal items) and different payment terms and free freight (to promote larger order value).

Case #4: Item Variants in Wholesale Distribution   The Distribution company carried several product lines involving item variants, ranging from t-shirts (with color and size variants) to industrial hardware (lengths, finish, and head type for variants of bolts and screws). Authorized variants were defined for each item, and SKU planning data defined for each item variant. The sales prices were different for each variant code, and for selling each variant code in different units of measure. For example, a lower price was offered for buying t-shirts in dozens. The sales price and line discount worksheets included the item variant code and sales UM to reflect these variations.

Case #5: Replacement Parts for Equipment   The Equipment company stocks and sells purchased material that serves as replacement parts (or service parts) for previously sold equipment. These purchased materials are also used in manufacturing the equipment. A separate location was defined for the service parts function, and each replacement part had two authorized locations—one for manufacturing and one for the service parts function. The SKUs for the separate service parts location had separate planning data reflecting min-max quantities to support customer service objectives.

Case #6: Actual Costing for Fabricated Products   The Fabricated Products company purchased several commodities such as precious metals with purchase prices that varied widely on a day-to-day basis. A FIFO actual costing method was assigned to these items, and the vendor invoice information was entered upon material receipt to keep actual costs up-to-date.

Executive Summary

Information about purchased material represents the heart of a distribution environment, and a significant portion of cost of sales for most manufacturing environments. Information about purchased material can be segmented into company-wide information (such as the item number, quality management policies, and sales data) and location-specific data (such as planning data to replenish inventory). Several factors must be considered in item identification such as units of measure and alternative identifiers for sales and purchasing purposes. Other considerations include approaches to the item description and item-related text. Quality management policies include lot- and serial-tracking requirements as well as approved vendors. Sales data involves defining item prices and discount percentages and possibly substitute items. Costing data for purchased material includes standard and actual costing methods, and vendor agreements about purchase prices and discounts. Location-specific planning data for purchased material includes a lead-time and reordering policy. Other types of items may be sold, such as item variants, non-stock items, and kit items. The case studies highlight variations in distribution environments, such as daily usage rates and rules-based pricing.

Chapter 3

Manufactured Items

A manufactured item requires product structure information defined by a bill of material and optional routing. Bill of material information defines the product design for a manufactured item, and provides the basis for product costing, material planning, material usage reporting, lot- and serial-tracking, and tracking progress through stages of manufacturing. Routing information defines the process design for a manufactured item, and provides the basis for calculating value-added costs, determining capacity requirements, scheduling production activities, reporting actual work performed and unit completions, and tracking progress of production activities.

The concept of a master bill and a master routing are used to define product structure. Each master bill has a unique identifier (termed a *production BOM number*) and specifies material components. Each master routing has a unique identifier (termed a *routing number*) and specifies operations. The master bill and routing are defined independently from any parent item, and their identifiers are subsequently assigned to items to define product structure. This approach is different than directly defining a bill and routing for a manufactured item. It is especially applicable for items with the same process design or the same drawing number, and for handling phantoms used in multiple products. The master bill and routing represent company-wide information.

Each manufactured item and its components must be defined in the item master. Item master information for purchased material was covered in the previous chapter. The item master information that uniquely applies to a manufactured item provides the starting point for further explanation

Item Master Information for Manufactured Items

Manufactured items are designated by the replenishment system policy (with a value of production order) that determines whether planning and costing calculations recognize an item's bill and routing. Information about a manufactured item can be segmented into company-wide and location-specific.

			Item	Stockkeeping Unit (SKU)
		Identifier	Item Number	Item Number + Location
Company-Wide	Planning Data	Master Bill	Defined As Company-Wide Information	/////
		Master Routing		/////
		Scrap Percent		/////
		Rounding Precision		/////
	Cost Data	Manufacturing Overhead		/////
		Standard Cost Calculation		/////
		Accounting Lot Size		/////
Location-Specific		Last Direct Cost	Define by Item (acts as the default value for the SKU)	Define by SKU (with initial default value from item)
	Planning Data	Inventory Posting Group		
		Replenishment System		
		Item Lead-Time		
		Manufacturing Policy		
		Flushing Method		
		Source of Components	/////	Define by SKU

Figure 3.1   Company-Wide vs. Location-Specific Manufacturing
Information

The previous chapter explained company-wide information for material (such as item numbering, quality data, and sales data) as well as location-specific information (such as planning data). The same considerations apply to manufactured material and will not be repeated here. However, there are several unique characteristics of manufactured items. These unique characteristics are summarized in Figure 3.1 and explained below in terms of company-wide and location-specific information.

Company-Wide Information for a Manufactured Item

The company-wide information includes the item number and several fields related to planning and cost data that are unique to manufactured items. Further explanation covers the significance of each field.

Item Number   The item number provides a unique internal identifier for each manufactured item, up to 20 characters in length. Any stage in the manufacturing process that can be stocked (or sold or purchased complete) requires an item number. While routing operations are generally used to reflect various steps in the manufacturing process, the stocking level consideration may mandate a separate item (with its own bill of material) for a given step. A production environment requiring an outside operation, for example, often defines one item number for each unfinished item sent to the subcontractor and a separate item number for the completed item The approach to defining a phantom component (using a master bill identifier as the component) does not require a separate item number for a phantom, but many firms assign an item number to the phantom to support item-related information.

Manufactured items may involve other considerations, such as the significance of revision levels and engineering drawing numbers, and units of measure for components and master bills.

- *Significance of Revision Level.* An item's revision level generally represents a level of documentation, and several terms (such as engineering change level) refer to the same concept. The significance of an item's revision level differs among manufacturers, especially in terms of a change in form, fit, or function and the impact on interchangeability. One viewpoint treats revision levels as interchangeable, and revision level can be treated as an item or bill attribute for reference purposes. A slight variation considers revision level to be different versions of a bill or routing, but the item's revision levels are still interchangeable. A second viewpoint considers revision level as part of the item's unique identifier, such as embedding it in the item number.

- *Significance of Drawing Number.* An item's drawing number often serves as the basis for the item number. It sometimes represents an attribute of the item. It may serve as the identifier for the item's master bill, especially when the same drawing (master bill) applies to multiple items.

- *UM Considerations for Manufactured Items.* Unit of measure considerations apply to component quantities, since a component quantity can be defined for a component-specific UM. The typical examples involve process manufacturing, such as an ingredient with a base UM of kilogram but a component quantity expressed in grams or milligrams. An additional UM consideration includes the specified UM for a master bill.

Master Bill of Material A master bill of material defines the components to produce an item. Planning and costing calculations, and the creation of order-dependent bills, are based on the master bill assigned to an item. The master bill identifies material components for building the item at any location.

Master Routing A master routing defines the routing operations to produce an item. Planning and costing calculations, and the creation of order-dependent routings, are based on the master routing assigned to an item. The master routing identifies work centers for building the item at a given location.

Scrap Percent A manufactured item's scrap percentage represents the additional requirements for components and routing operation time to produce the item.

Rounding Precision   A component's rounding precision can help avoid confusion when a fractional quantity in the bill results in a fractional quantity in a production order pick list. For example, a component with a fractional quantity per of .33333, and a production order quantity of 100 would result in a requirement to issue 33.333 units. The rounding precision should be 0 when the component's base UM is pieces (so that 34 pieces should be issued in the example), or it might be 2 when the component's base UM is kilograms (so that 33.34 kg should be issued).

Manufacturing Overhead   Item-related overhead costs are expressed as an amount or percentage or both, and provide the basis for calculating manufacturing overhead for a manufactured item.

Standard Cost Calculation   The standard costs for a manufactured item are calculated based on the master bill and routing data, the item's scrap percentage and overhead factors, and the item's accounting lot size. A manufacturing setup policy determines whether setup costs should be included or excluded from costing calculations.

Accounting Lot Size   Cost roll-up calculations use an item's accounting lot size (termed lot size) to amortize routing-related fixed costs, such as an operation's setup time and fixed scrap quantity. The SKU's lot size is ignored in cost roll-up calculations, but it is used for suppressing suggested action messages about insignificant quantity changes (based on a percent of lot size quantity).

Location-Specific Information for a Manufactured Item

The authorized locations for building and stocking a manufactured item are identified as SKUs.[1] Each SKU defines location-specific information that includes several fields unique to a manufactured item (such as manufacturing policy). It also includes several fields that have a different significance (such as item lead-time) for a manufactured item. These fields have been grouped into planning and costing data in Figure 3.1, and further explanation covers the significance of each field.

---

[1] The concept of an authorized location only affects the ability to have location-specific information such as planning data. It does not affect the ability to create a production order for the item at other locations.

Replenishment System   The SKU's replenishment system indicates the item is manufactured at the location or transferred to the location from another site. Note that the item's replenishment system (a company-wide policy) determines whether standard cost roll-up calculations recognize an item's bill and routing.

Lead-Time   The SKU's lead-time provides a fixed production lead-time (when routing data does not exist) for manufacturing product at the location. This chapter's section, "Planning Data for Suggested Production Orders," describes how routing data can be used to calculate a variable production lead-time.

Manufacturing Policy   An SKU's manufacturing policy—either make-to-stock or make-to-order—determines how the system creates production orders for the location. Production orders for a make-to-order SKU, for example, are typically linked to a sales order. This chapter's section, "Planning Data for Suggested Production Orders," provides further explanation of the manufacturing policy.

Flushing Method   A flushing method applies to reporting item usage as a component: it can be manually issued or auto-deducted from stock. This chapter's section, "Methods for Reporting Component Usage," provides further explanation of flushing methods.

Last Direct Cost   The SKU's last direct cost gets updated after the status of a production order (at the location) has been changed to finished.

Inventory Posting Group   The inventory posting group assigned to an item reflects several location-specific account numbers critical for a manufactured item, such as the accounts for production order variances and work-in-process inventory.

Source of Components   The source of components (termed the *components at location* field) only applies to certain multisite operations but it is explained here for continuity's sake. Components are normally located at the same location as the production order for the parent item, but some multisite operations require an exception to this rule. Two examples will help clarify this exception. One example involves a manufacturing plant and a separate service parts location, where production orders in the service parts location use components stocked at the manufacturing plant. A second example involves a manufacturing plant with an adjoining raw material warehouse treated as a separate location; components for production orders are issued directly from the adjoining warehouse. These two examples could be modeled using the SKU's components at location field to indicate the alternate source of components. Alternatively, a company-wide setup policy could define the source of components. In either case, the specified source of components enables planning calculations to correctly interpret requirements for replenishing inventory.

Bills of Material

A master bill of material defines the components required to produce a manufactured item. It may optionally have one or more bill versions. The master bill (and bill version if applicable) provides the initial basis for components in an order-dependent bill. The following sections review the creation and use of master bills and the component information.

Master Bill of Material

The identifier for a master bill of material (termed *production BOM number*) can be automatically or manually assigned. When a manufacturer employs a unique bill for each item, manual assignment can be used to match the identifier to the applicable parent item number or the item's drawing number. Most users find the significant identifier easier to use than an auto-assigned identifier. After defining a master bill and its components, the master bill identifier must be assigned to the relevant item number(s).

A master bill has a separate status that affects bill maintenance and usability. The *certified* status indicates the master bill has been completely defined, prevents maintenance of component information, and enables the bill to be used for costing and planning purposes. A status of *new, under development,* or *closed* allows maintenance of component information, but prevents cost roll-up and planning calculations as well as creation of a production order.

Each master bill must have a specified UM so that component-required quantities reflect the quantity per unit. This requirement for a specified UM stems from how a master bill decouples the relationship between a parent item and its bill components. Most manufacturing environments use a specified UM that matches the base UM for the parent item. The specified UM supports those environments requiring production in a different UM or bills that vary by lot size.

Components in a Master Bill of Material

A component in a master bill is termed a *BOM line*. Information for each component includes the component type, component item, required quantity, planned scrap percentage, find number, routing link code, and effectivity dates.

Component Type and Component Item   The component type indicates whether the component is a normal item (defined by an item number) or a phantom (defined by a master bill identifier). This approach to phantoms means that an item number is not required for a phantom, although some firms define an item to indicate attributes (such as drawing number) or handle sales of the phantom. This phantom approach also means that blow-though logic only applies to material components and ignores a phantom's inventory. A blank component type can be used to indicate comments in the component description field.

Component Required Quantity   A component's required quantity reflects the amount needed to build one parent item, using the master bill's specified UM. This *quantity per* can be entered as a fraction or decimal, with a limit of five decimal places. The component's required quantity normally reflects its base UM, but a different UM can be specified for the component. The component's UM provides one approach to handling more than five decimal places in a required quantity, such as expressing .123456 kilograms as 123.456 grams.

A special case of component required quantity involves a calculation formula based on quantity per and dimensions such as length, width, depth, or weight. With cut-to-size material, for example, a component requirement for steel rod could be specified as three pieces of two-foot lengths, resulting in a total requirement of six feet. This approach avoids the need for creating different item numbers for unique sizes and provides the basis for communicating cut-to-size instructions to production.

By-Products and a Negative Component Quantity

A negative quantity for a bill component represents a by-product component. Cost roll-up calculations subtract the cost for a by-product component. Planning calculations recognize the scheduled receipt for a by-product component. The order-dependent bill for a production order includes the by-product component, and a by-product component can be manually added to the order-dependent bill. A by-product component in the order-dependent bill can be received into inventory from the production order (via the *Consumption Journal* window used to issue other components). Differences between standard and actual by-product receipts are treated as a material variance.

Planned Scrap Percentage   A component's planned scrap percentage indicates that normal manufacturing practices result in scrapped components. Other approaches can be used to identify planned scrap as described in the following breakout box.

Identifying Planned Manufacturing Scrap

Planned manufacturing scrap can be expressed with several different approaches. A planned scrap percentage for an individual bill component will increase its requirements on an order-dependent bill and in planning calculations. A planned scrap percentage for a parent item will increase requirements for all of its components and operations. The planned scrap percentage and fixed scrap quantity for an individual routing operation will increase requirements for its total operation time and for related material components, and have an additive effect on previous operations in a multistep routing. Each scrap approach will also be considered in cost roll-up calculations for parent items.

Routing Link Code   A routing link code assigned to a routing operation can also be assigned to relevant components in the bill. This ensures that material due dates reflect the operation start date, material requirements reflect the operation scrap factors, and auto-deduction of material components can be tied to unit completions reported for the operation. The routing link code is optional.

Production Lead-Time   A component may be required a number of days prior to (or after) the production order start date, or the operation start date when the material is linked to the operation. A positive production lead-time indicates a requirement before the start date, whereas a negative value indicates a requirement after the start date.

Effectivity Dates   A component's starting and ending dates indicate planned changes to a bill of material. Phasing out an existing component on date X and phasing in a new component on date X+1, for example, would indicate a planned replacement. These component effectivity dates are used in planning calculations, cost roll-up calculations, and creation of an order-dependent bill.

Bill-Related Text   Comments can be entered for a component or for the master bill. Text can also be entered as a separate component line using a component type of *blank.*

Position Information for a Material Component   Position information provides reference data that can serve different purposes. Some manufacturers employ a position number to represent a sequential counter of components, often tied to the find number on drawings. Some firms use the position field(s) to identify a grouping of components, such as the material needed for an operation (when routing data isn't used), the delivery area for a group of picked components, or a group representing related parts in the production process. A few firms use the position fields to identify the in-revision and out-revision of each component. The position fields provide one approach for handling reference designators.

Versions of a Master Bill

A master bill can optionally have additional versions, where each version has a unique identifier termed a *version number*. Some manufacturing environments employ versions of a bill to manage planned engineering changes, to define authorized recipes, or to serve some other purpose. Each bill version requires the same information as a master bill, such as status and specified UM, and the same component information. Each version defines a unique bill of material and multiple versions can exist, each with a certified status. The desired version of a bill can be manually specified on a production order.

Each version also has a starting date field. The starting date is optional and provides one approach to planned engineering changes. Each version's starting date determines when it becomes active, and bill versions supercede each other automatically. Bill versions can be compared. The active bill version acts as the default on production orders, but it can be manually overridden.

Copying a Bill of Material

Components in a master bill can be manually entered or automatically created by copying components from another master bill. After using the copy bill function, the system incrementally adds the new components to the existing components. The copy bill function can be used multiple times to generate incremental additions. The components can then be manually maintained.

Components in a version of the master bill can also be created via copying. Components can be copied from the master bill or another version of the master bill. After using the copy function, the system deletes existing components and adds the new components. The copy bill approach for bill versions does not support incremental additions.

Order-Dependent Bills

An order-dependent bill (termed *production order components*) refers to the bill of material attached to a production order. Changes to an order-dependent bill do not affect the master bill. Creation and maintenance of an order-dependent bill reflects several rules. These rules include:

1. The refresh process for a production order can delete the existing order-dependent bill and replace it with a new one.

2. When an order-dependent bill is initially created, it reflects the bill version (if applicable) and components in effect as of the production order due date. The user can optionally override the master bill and/or the bill version on a production order prior to creating the order-dependent bill.

3. The order-dependent bill contains components of a phantom.

4. The user can modify the components in an order-dependent bill to indicate material substitutions, additions, deletions, and quantity changes. A component's flushing method can be changed.

5. An order-dependent bill can be created for a firm planned and released production order as well as a simulated production order. It can also be created for a planned production order, but planned orders get automatically deleted by planning calculations.

6. A released production order cannot be refreshed after reporting material or capacity usage against the order.

7. An order-dependent bill applies to each line in a multiline production order.

A material item can be issued to a released production order even when the component does not exist on the order-dependent bill; it does not get added to the order-dependent bill.

Methods for Reporting Component Usage

Component usage can be manually reported or auto-deducted for a production order. Many manufacturers prefer manual reporting because it provides a method for inventory control, they have lot- or serial-controlled components, or they perceive auto-deduction as too complex. The manual reporting approach requires more transaction processing, but automated data collection can minimize this impact.

Auto-deduction reflects the component quantity defined in the order-dependent bill. Auto-deduction logic can be forward or backward and considers whether a component is linked to an operation via a routing link code.

◆ For non-linked components, changing a production order's status to *released* triggers forward flushing while changing status to *finished* triggers backward flushing. Forward deduction reflects the production order quantity (also termed the theoretical output quantity) while backward flushing reflects the actual output quantity reported.

♦ For a linked component, starting the operation triggers forward deduction while reporting unit completion triggers backward deduction. Forward deduction reflects the theoretical units for the operation while backward flushing reflects the actual output units for the operation.

Auto-deduction of a component's inventory requires information about where it is located. The order-dependent bill identifies the location and bin that will be used for auto-deducting a component. The component's location normally reflects the manufacturing location specified for the production order; the component's bin reflects its default bin within the location. This means each component item must have inventory in its default bin for auto-deduction purposes.

Manual reporting can be used to identify additional material usage after a component has been auto-deducted. An auto-deduction approach requires accurate bills, and accurate routing data about linking codes, to be effective.

The method for reporting a component's usage is termed a *flushing method* and is defined on the item master. The SKU's flushing method acts as the default when the item is a component on an order-dependent bill. The flushing method can be overridden at this point.

Work Centers and Machines

Operations can be performed at a machine or work center, and these represent company-wide information. Machines can be grouped into work centers for the purpose of calculating consolidated capacity. As a general guideline, either machines or work centers should be used when defining routing operations. This approach avoids unnecessary confusion in specifying costs and available capacity, and recognizes the limitations about automatically scheduling operations on machines within a work center. Further explanations focus on using work centers.

A work center may represent an internal resource or an external subcontractor. Both types of work centers have a physical identity and operate under capacity constraints, expressed in hours of operation (such as 7 a.m. to 4 p.m.). Internal and external work centers can be conceptualized similarly, but differ significantly in terms of costing, time requirements, and scheduling logic.

Internal Work Centers

Information about an internal work center includes the identifier, the assignment to a work center group, the work center's UM, available capacity, and costs. The scheduling of production orders in a work center normally reflects an infinite loading viewpoint, but a finite loading viewpoint applies to work centers designated as capacity constrained

Work Center Identification A work center number uniquely identifies each internal and external work center. The identification of internal work centers generally reflects the layout of a manufacturing plant, such as identifying a manufacturing cell, groups of similar machines, or groups of people with similar skills. Additional considerations may include the amount of detail needed for defining process specifications, the similarity of costing data, and the need for capacity planning and separate production schedules. These considerations must be balanced against the amount of effort to define and maintain routing data.

In a multisite operation, the exact same piece of equipment (or manufacturing cell) in two locations must be defined by two different work center identifiers.

Work Center Group A work center group typically represents a department and one group is assigned to each work center. The cumulative load and available capacity can be viewed for each work center group, thereby supporting aggregate capacity planning across multiple work centers.

In a multisite operation, the work center group can represent similar equipment in multiple locations, so that aggregate capacity planning supports centralized master scheduling. In this way, production could be shifted between locations to avoid an overloaded work center.

Work Center Capacity and UM Work center capacity and costs are expressed in a time-based unit of measure, such as hours, minutes, or days. Most firms use hours for all work centers, or at least a consistent UM for all work centers within a work center group. The work center's UM acts as a default for expressing time requirements in routing operations performed at the work center. However, an operation's time requirements can be expressed in a different UM such as minutes.

A work center's available capacity reflects its hours of operation and the average number of machines (or people) that can be working during these hours. The number of machines (or people) is termed the capacity of the work center. A manufacturing cell or an assembly line typically has a capacity of one regardless of how many people or machines are involved in its operation.

The assigned shop calendar defines the hours of operation for a work center. Each shop calendar defines a repeating pattern of working days and working hours per day, with optional holiday exceptions expressed in terms of specific dates. The available capacity can be adjusted by an efficiency percentage assigned to the work center. A separate function calculates a work center's available hours over a user-defined time horizon, where the calculations reflect the assigned shop calendar, holidays, efficiency percentage, and the average number of machines (or people).

Work Center Costs and UM   A work center's costs are expressed per its UM, such as costs per hour of operation. A work center's costs consist of a direct unit cost and overhead cost, where overhead costs can be expressed using an amount or a percentage (of direct unit cost) or both. The direct unit cost and overhead cost comprise two cost elements termed *capacity* cost and *capacity overhead* cost. The system uses these two cost elements in cost roll-up calculations and for charging time reported at the work center. These two cost elements also provide the basis for calculating production order variances related to capacity and capacity overhead.

Infinite vs. Finite Loading Viewpoints   A work center is normally treated as having infinite capacity for scheduling purposes, such as calculating an operation's elapsed time and a production order's lead-time. Scheduling logic ignores current loads, which means an unlimited number of orders can be scheduled concurrently at a work center for each operation's duration. An analysis of work center load versus capacity can be used to identify overloaded periods, so that manual adjustments can be made to loads or available capacity.

A work center can optionally be designated as a *finite* or a *capacity constrained resource*. Scheduling logic considers current loads, which means a single order can be scheduled at the work center for the operation's duration. Scheduling logic considers two additional factors when loading a capacity constrained resource: a load percentage (relative to available capacity) that limits the amount loaded and a tolerance percentage that allows overloading. A firm's bottleneck work centers are typically identified as a capacity constrained resource.

External Work Centers

An external work center represents a single vendor performing an outside operation on supplied material. Each outside operation in a routing specifies an external work center that has a designated vendor. Definition of an external work center is similar to an internal work center, with several major exceptions.

- An external work center has a designated vendor as the subcontractor. The designated vendor acts as a default for suggested purchases for outside operations.
- Costs are specified for each routing operation performed by an external work center, typically expressed per unit. This unit cost represents a *subcontract* cost element in cost roll-up calculations, and acts as a default purchase price on suggested purchases.
- The external work center is assigned a shop calendar that reflects the vendor's hours of operation. Scheduling logic uses this shop calendar, along with the time requirements for an outside operation, to schedule the turnaround time at the subcontractor.

Summarized Information for a Work Center

A work center's statistics summarize available capacity, actual reported time, and a capacity utilization percentage for the current accounting period, current year to date, and the preceding year. A work center's load window summarizes available capacity, expected load, and a capacity utilization percentage for various time increments, such as months and weeks. It also provides drill down to the production orders causing the expected load.

Routings

A master routing defines the operations required to produce a manufactured item. It may optionally have one or more routing versions. The master routing (and routing version if applicable) provides the initial basis for operations in an order-dependent routing. The following sections review the creation and use of master routings and the information about internal and external operations.

Master Routing

The identifier for a master routing (termed a *routing number*) can be automatically or manually assigned. When a manufacturer employs a unique routing for each item, manual assignment can be used to match the identifier to the applicable parent item. Some manufacturers employ a common routing for producing different items; the common routing approach reduces routing maintenance efforts. After defining a master routing and its operations, the master routing identifier must be assigned to the relevant item number(s).

A master routing has a separate status that affects routing maintenance and usability. The *certified* status indicates the master routing has been completely defined, prevents maintenance of routing operations, and enables the routing to be used for costing and scheduling purposes. A status of *new, under development,* or *closed* allows maintenance of component information, but prevents cost roll-up and planning calculations as well as creation of a production order.

A master routing does not have a specified UM, unlike a master bill. The run times for each operation represent the quantity per parent item for an implied unit of measure.

Each master routing has a routing type—serial versus parallel—indicating how operation sequences should be treated for scheduling purposes. Scheduling logic is based on operation sequence numbers in a serial routing. In a routing with one or more parallel operations, scheduling logic must be based on user-specified values for the previous and/or next operation sequence number assigned to each operation.

Internal Operations in a Master Routing

Information about each internal operation (termed a *routing detail line*) includes the operation sequence number, time requirements, scrap factors, routing link code, and other information. Most companies will use either work centers or machines in their routing data; we will simplify the explanation by focusing on work centers.

Operation Sequence Number   The operation sequence number provides a unique identifier for each operation within a routing, and provides the basis for scheduling a serial routing. For a parallel routing, scheduling logic requires additional information about the operation sequence numbers for previous and/or next operations. A routing containing several serial operations and only one parallel operation is still considered a parallel routing.

Time Requirements   Time requirements for an operation typically consist of run time per unit and optional setup time. Time can be expressed in an operation-specific UM, including a run rate such as 100 units per hour. Cost calculations are based on run time and setup time, although setup time can be optionally excluded.

Other time requirements may be specified for scheduling purposes. A wait time represents a drying or cooling period after completing an operation, while move time represents the time an item spends in transit from one operation to another. Scheduling logic uses the setup, run, wait, and move time plus the queue time for each relevant work center to calculate lead-time for a production order.

Scrap Factors   Operation scrap can be expressed as a variable (percentage) or a fixed amount or both. The operation scrap factors have a cumulative effect in a multistep routing.

Routing Link Code   A routing link code assigned to a routing operation can also be assigned to relevant components in the bill. This ensures that material due dates reflect the operation start date, material requirements reflect the operation scrap factors, and auto-deduction of material components can be tied to unit completions reported for the operation. The user-defined link codes often correspond to work centers where material usage occurs.

Other Scheduling Information   Other scheduling information includes a send-ahead quantity and a concurrent processing quantity. A send-ahead quantity models overlapping operations, where the next operation can be started after production of the send-ahead quantity. A concurrent processing quantity indicates that multiple machines or people can work on the operation to reduce the elapsed run time. Scheduling information for a parallel routing also includes the operation sequence numbers for the previous and/or next operations.

Other Descriptive Information   Descriptive information about an operation includes comments, tools, and quality measures. Descriptive information can also be predefined as a standard task code, and then reused in routing operations.

External Operations in a Master Routing

Information about each outside operation differs slightly from an internal operation. The primary differences involve the work center, the unit cost per item, and time requirements.

- *Work Center.* The specified external work center has an associated vendor. Costs are not typically specified for an external work center, and a costing policy (termed *specific unit cost*) indicates that costs are specified at the operation level in terms of a cost per unit.
- *Unit Cost per Item.* The specified unit cost per item reflects the purchase price of the outside operation and a subcontract cost element.
- *Time Requirements.* Time requirements for the external work center typically consist of a move time to indicate the elapsed turnaround time for the outside operation. The appropriate value depends on how available capacity is defined in the work center's shop calendar. For example, a three-day turnaround time could be expressed as 24 hours move time when the work center's shop calendar contains 8 hours per day.

An outside operation involves two streams of supply chain activities—for the production order operation and its related purchase order—that require coordination. Creating a released production order results in an order-dependent routing with the outside operation, and a suggested purchase can be identified for the outside operation. The suggested purchase identifies the relevant production order and operation sequence, along with a suggested purchase price, vendor, quantity, and turnaround time.

There are two different approaches regarding component material for an outside operation: the component material can be issued as a kit or stocked at the vendor. The selected approach impacts how to model material consumption.

- *Issuing Components as a Kit.* The supplied material is issued against the production order and the completed items are received against the purchase order.
- *Stocking Components at the Vendor.* The consumption of component material still needs to be reported against the production order (typically through backward flushing), and the completed items are received against the purchase order.

In either case, actual costs are passed directly to the production order's operation upon purchase order receipt. When the outside operation is the last operation in the routing, the output must be reported to receive the completed parent item into inventory. Otherwise, the reporting of operation time and/or unit completions against the production order is not typically required for an outside operation.

Versions of a Master Routing

A master routing can optionally have additional versions, where each version has a unique identifier termed a *version number*. Each routing version requires the same information as a master routing, such as status and routing type, and the same operation information. Each version defines a unique routing and multiple versions can exist, each with a certified status. The desired version of a routing can be manually specified on a production order.

Each version also has an optional starting date field that supports planned engineering changes. Each version's starting date determines when it becomes active, and the system automatically recognizes superceding routing versions and the active version. The active routing version acts as the default on production orders, but it can be manually overridden.

Order-Dependent Routings

An order-dependent routing (termed a *production order routing*) refers to the routing operations attached to a production order. Changes to an order-dependent routing do not affect the master routing, and typically reflect an alternate operation. The previously described rules for creation and maintenance of an order-dependent bill also apply to an order-dependent routing. However, time can only be reported when the operation sequence exists in the order-dependent bill.

An operation in the order-dependent routing can be flagged for manual scheduling, thereby preventing automatic calculation of production lead time based on routing data.

Methods for Reporting Time at a Work Center

Actual work center time expended on a routing operation can be manually reported or auto-deducted. Manually reported time reflects the operation's unit of measure such as minutes or hours, and can be recorded along with unit completions for the operation.

Auto-deduction reflects the operation time defined in the order-dependent routing. Auto-deduction logic can be forward or backward, representing auto-deduction at the start or finish of a production order. Changing a production order's status to *released* triggers forward flushing while changing status to *finished* triggers backward flushing. Forward flushing reflects the production order quantity while backward flushing reflects the actual output reported. Manual reporting can be used to identify additional time expended after an operation's time has been auto-deducted.

The method for reporting time at a work center (termed a *flushing method*) is defined on the work center master. This flushing method acts as the default for an operation component on an order-dependent routing, where it can be overridden.

Maintaining Bills and Routings

Maintenance of bills and routings can employ several tools for analyzing and changing information. Planned engineering changes to product and process design can also be identified.

Managing Planned Engineering Changes

Planned engineering changes to master bills can be identified using two different approaches—start date effectivity for bill versions and start/end date effectivity for bill components—or a combined approach. Planned engineering changes to master routings can only be identified using one approach: the start date effectivity for routing versions. The due date of a production order determines which components, bill version, and routing version will be used as the basis for requirements and the creation of an order-dependent bill and routing.

The master bill and routing, as well as the bill version and routing version, can be manually overridden on a production order line item.

Some engineering changes require immediate implementation and updates to existing production orders. When no activity has been reported, a production order can be *refreshed* to obtain the latest information defined in the master bills and routings. When activity has been reported, the user must manually update the order-dependent bill and routing on existing production orders.

The status field for a master bill and routing provides one approach to indicate whether it has been certified as complete or is still under development. However, some firms must work with partially defined bills to calculate requirements for long lead-time materials or to perform preliminary cost calculations. Planning and cost roll-up calculations only work with certified bills and routings.

Tools for Maintaining and Analyzing Bills and Routings

Several approaches make bill maintenance easier, such as copying a master bill (or a version of a master bill) and changing one component with another. A master routing (or version of a master routing) can also be copied. The system prevents circular bills. However, an item can be made out of itself when using a production order for rework purposes; the order-dependent bill identifies the item as a component to make the same item.

Analysis tools include online inquires about a component where-used, a master bill where-used, and a comparison of components in multiple versions of a master bill. Standard reports include a costed bill and a comparison between two master bills as of a specified date. Other analysis tools include a where-used inquiry for a master routing.

Planning Data for Suggested Production Orders

Production orders are typically created based on a system-generated suggestion for material replenishment. The replenishment suggestions reflect planning data for a manufactured item, including the primary source of supply, lead-time, reordering policy, and manufacturing policy. Suggestions can be directed to the planner responsible for the item. The previous chapter covered these same planning data for purchased material.

Planner Responsibility

The concept of planner responsibility provides an organizing focus for communicating the need to synchronize supplies with demands. By assigning planner responsibility to items and production orders, suggested action messages can be directed to the responsible planner. Two approaches to indicate planner responsibility are illustrated below.

- *General Product Posting Group Field.* Using this field to indicate planner responsibility, suggested actions about new and existing production orders can be directed to the planner. It can be optionally overridden on a production order to indicate a change in planner responsibility.
- *Product Group Code Field.* Using this field to indicate planner responsibility achieves the same results as above.

Chapter 8 provides further explanation of suggested action messages about production orders.

Primary Source of Supply

The primary source of supply for a manufactured item is indicated by the replenishment system policy and by the identifiers for a master bill and master routing.

Production Lead-Time

Production lead-time can be variable or fixed depending on whether routing data exists. Routing data reflects the item's master routing for a new order; it reflects the order-dependent routing for an existing order. The system calculates a variable lead-time based on the routing data; otherwise it uses the fixed lead-time specified for the SKU. The SKU's fixed lead-time is typically expressed in the average number of working days required to produce an average order quantity under average factory load conditions.

Production Lead-Time and Capable-to-Promise Logic

Capable-to-promise (CTP) logic provides one approach to making sales order delivery promises and an approximation of forward finite scheduling. CTP logic calculates the lead-time to produce an item, and the lead-time for components marked as *critical,* to determine an item's earliest ship date. Production lead-time may be fixed or variable (based on routing data). Calculations for a variable lead-time reflect the routing operations factored by order quantity, available capacity of relevant work centers, and loading for each work center based on its infinite or finite capacity viewpoint.

The lead-time for a critical component depends on its primary source. The system uses production lead-time for a manufactured item and purchasing lead-time for a purchased item. A multisite operation may also have items sourced from another location where the component has a transportation lead-time.

Reordering Policy

A reordering policy and order modifiers represent a model of the planner's decision-making logic concerning production quantity and reorder cycle. The five replenishment methods for purchased material, explained in the previous chapter, also apply to manufactured items.

Manufacturing Policy

The manufacturing policy determines whether suggested replenishment via production orders will be directly or indirectly linked to sales orders. It also guides selection of an appropriate reordering policy and planning parameters. The implications for a make-to-stock and a make-to-order manufacturing policy are summarized below.

- *Make-to-Stock Manufacturing Policy.* This policy applies to a stocked item where suggested production orders are indirectly linked to demands via dates. The SKU's reordering policies should reflect time-phased order point or MRP logic, with optional use of order modifiers.

- *Make-to-Order Manufacturing Policy.* This policy applies to manufactured items produced to customer demand where suggested production orders are directly linked to sales orders. The reordering policy typically reflects order-driven logic. A suggested production order automatically reflects changes in the sales order quantity, shipment date, and ship-from location, but manual changes are required after taking action to firm or release the suggested production order.

A make-to-order manufactured product may consist of a multilevel product structure where lower-level components are also produced to customer demand. When these manufactured components are also designated as make-to-order, the suggested production order consists of multiple lines, one for the end-item and one for each make-to-order component. This is termed a multiline production order, and scheduled dates for each line item reflect the product structure dependencies.

> ### Methods for Establishing Direct Linkage Between
> ### Production Orders and a Sales Order

The make-to-order manufacturing policy provides one approach (using the planning calculations) to generate a suggested production order directly linked to a sales order. There are two other methods.

- A production order can be directly generated from a sales order regardless of its manufacturing policy. The system automatically creates a separate production order corresponding to each sales order line item for a manufactured item. It also generates an additional line item for each of the manufactured item's components designated as make-to-order. The user can alternatively choose to generate a single production order (termed a project order) with multiple lines that correspond to the sales order line items.

- An item's production order can be manually entered and linked to an existing sales order regardless of its manufacturing policy. The user can manually assign an order number that matches the sales order number. The system generates a multiline production order when the sales order has multiple lines. An additional line is created for each of the manufactured item's components designated as make-to-order.

The production order initially reflects the sales order quantity, shipment date, and ship-from location, but it can be scheduled independently. With a firm planned or released production order, changes to the sales order (and sales order deletion) require a separate manual update to the production order.

Other Planning Data

The scrap percent for a manufactured item increases the required quantity for all components and routing operations. A safety stock quantity and a safety lead-time can also be specified.

Standard Cost Data for Manufactured Items

The standard costs for a manufactured item can be automatically calculated based on item, bill, and routing information. A manufactured item's standard costs consist of rolled costs and single-level costs, where both are segmented into cost elements for material, capacity, subcontract, capacity overhead, and manufacturing overhead.

Approaches to Cost Roll-Up Calculations

The system provides two different approaches to cost roll-up calculations, labeled for simplicity's sake as a direct update approach and a worksheet approach.

- *Direct Update Approach.* Cost roll-up calculations can be performed for a single item with an immediate update of its standard costs, using the bill and routing in effect as of the system work date. The approach can also be used to calculate and update standard costs for all items within the item's multilevel bill.

- *Worksheet Approach.* Each standard cost worksheet represents a separate set of cost data for performing cost roll-up calculations. A worksheet contains one or more items. Items can be manually or automatically added to the worksheet, and the system copies each item's standard costs into the worksheet. Work centers can also be manually or automatically added to the worksheet, with a copy of their standard costs. Different costs can be entered for purchased material and work centers, and cost roll-up calculations performed as of a specified date. The worksheet displays the new calculated costs as well as the existing standard costs. The new calculated costs within the worksheet can be optionally copied into the standard costs for the specified items and work centers.

A worksheet has a unique identifier, and multiple worksheets can be defined. For example, one worksheet may represent next year's standard costs while another represents a simulation. The worksheet approach provides a method for preparing and entering mass changes to standard costs, such as periodic updates that reflect roll-up calculations as of a specified date.

Information Used in Cost Roll-Up Calculations

Cost roll-up calculations utilize data from several sources, where the source defines how to categorize costs into cost elements.

- *Items.* Each purchased component defines a standard cost that is treated as a material cost element. A manufactured item may have overhead costs, expressed as an amount and/or a percentage, that are treated as a manufacturing overhead cost element. A manufacturing item can also have a scrap percentage and an accounting lot size for amortizing fixed costs.

- *Bills of Material.* Each component defines a quantity per, a component scrap percentage, and effectivity dates. Bill versions also identify a starting effectivity date.

- *Internal Work Centers.* Each work center defines standard costs for direct time and overhead that are treated as cost elements for capacity and capacity overhead, respectively.

- *Internal Routing Operations.* Each internal routing operation defines setup and run time within an internal work center. An operation may also identify planned manufacturing scrap either as a quantity or a percentage or both.

- *External Operations.* Each external operation typically specifies a cost per unit that is treated as a subcontract cost element. In some cases, hourly costs are specified for the external work center and run times specified for the external operation.

- *Company Policies.* Setup costs can be excluded from cost roll-up calculations for manufactured items. Setup costs reflect an operation's setup time and fixed scrap amount.

Single-Level and Rolled Costs

The rolled costs for a manufactured item are based on the item's entire product structure, and the system retains segmentation by cost element.

- Material costs represent bill requirements for all purchased components and each component's standard cost inclusive of material-related overheads.

- Capacity and capacity overhead costs represent the time requirements for all internal operations and the relevant work center's costs.

- Subcontract costs represent routing requirements for all external operations.

- Manufacturing overhead costs represent overheads specified for the manufactured items.

The sum of these cost elements defines the item's standard cost used in valuing inventory transactions and cost of sales. The sum of cost elements for single-level costs and rolled costs are equal. This is because the single-level costs treat all components as a material cost element whether they are purchased or manufactured.

Case Studies

Case #7: Virtual Manufacturing   One division of the All-and-Anything company was moving toward virtual manufacturing with outsourcing of almost all production activities. Items were either purchased complete or subcontracted (with supplied material linked to the outside operation). In both cases, the bill of materials required an additional component type (termed a *reference component*) to define components provided by the subcontractor.

With the subcontracted approach, the supplied material and finished goods inventory were stocked at the vendor's location. Purchased material was shipped directly to a subcontractor and sales orders were shipped directly from a subcontractor. Supplied material was auto-deducted based on reported completions and replenished based on SKU planning data. In some cases, the completed units were transferred back to a company location for further processing (such as final assembly and test) before sales order shipment.

Case #8: CAD Integration   The All-and-Anything company required integration between its computer-aided design (CAD) package and information about items, bills, and routings. For standard products, this involved importing bill information from the CAD package into the master bill and viewing the CAD drawing from selected windows. They used a rules-based configurator to define the bill for a custom product and calculate a quoted price and estimated costs. This configuration information could be used by their CAD package to generate 3D models (for viewing) and 2D layout drawings, and cut lists for assisting production personnel in completing the work. This integration helped reduce the elapsed time to prepare sales quotes, the man-hours to define drawings and bills, and the cost of errors (including production rework, field installation services, and customer confidence).[2]

Case #9: Authorized Recipes in Process Manufacturing   The Batch Process company produces batches of bulk chemical and immediately puts it in various bottles with labels and packaging material for each bottle. They have several authorized recipes for each product that reflect variations in batch size. They use bill versions to model authorized recipes, with a specified UM for each bill version indicating batch size.

Case #10: By-Products in Pharmaceutical Products   The Batch Process company produced a pharmaceutical product where the production process resulted in several by-products of lower potency. Each by-product was a different item number, and could be packaged and sold as a different item. The master bill identified each planned by-product as a negative component quantity. The component quantity expressed a ratio (such as .15) indicating the expected by-product output relative to the parent item output.

Case #11: Printed Circuit Boards   The Consumer Products company produced electrical products that required assembly of printed circuit

---

[2] See www.csbsystems.com for more information.

boards from components. Critical components, boards, and end-items require lot tracking and serialization of end-items upon shipment. Using customized bill functionality, the engineering function identified approved vendors for components and specified reference designators for placing components on printed circuit boards.

Case #12: Item Variants in Bills   The Consumer Products company purchased baseball hats in various colors and sizes, and then packaged them together (such as a 24-pack) with a mix of colors and sizes. They used item variants to identify the purchased hats, and a manufactured item for each package (such as the 24-pack). Variants of the purchased item were specified as the bill components of the manufactured item.

Case #13: Engineering Bills vs. Production Bills   The engineering department wanted to define a separate engineering bill and then convert it into a production bill of material. They defined a separate bill version for the engineering bill, and used the certified status to indicate it was ready for use by production. The scheduler defined a cut-over or start date for the new bill version that considered current inventories and other factors.

Case #14: Common Bill for Fabricated Subassemblies   The Equipment company produced different brackets that had identical bills of material, but differed in the number of holes drilled in the bracket. A master bill identified the common bill of material, and was designated as the bill for each bracket item.

Case #15: Cut-to-Size Raw Materials in Fabricated Products
The Fabricated Products company needed to express bill requirements in terms of the number pieces of cut-to-size raw materials, such as steel rod and sheet metal, but did not want to create item numbers for each unique size. They solved the problem using the calculation formula for a component's required quantity. For example, they used the component's required quantity to represent pieces, and the component's physical dimensions to indicate the desired length of steel rod. This approach identified purchasing and stockroom picking requirements for the raw materials, and provided cut-to-size instructions for production.

Case #16: By-Products in Fabricated Products Manufacturing   The Fabricated Products company produced plastic parts where the production process for plastic resulted in reusable scrap (identified by a unique item number) that could be melted down in subsequent runs. The reusable scrap represented a by-product that was identified in the master bill as a negative quantity, and received into stock as a result of a production order.

Executive Summary

Modeling supply chain activities for a manufactured item involves item master, bill of material, and optional routing information. The item master includes company-wide information (such as the item number and master bill identifier) and location-specific information (such as the planning data). A master bill defines the components to build a manufactured item. A master routing defines the work centers and operations—both internal and external—to build a manufactured item. Planned engineering changes to the master bill and routing can be specified, and each production order has an order-dependent bill and routing. Suggested production orders are based on location-specific planning data such as the production lead-time and reordering policy. In particular, a make-to-order manufacturing policy determines whether suggested production orders are linked to sales order demand. Standard costs for a manufactured item are calculated based on the item master, bill, and routing information. The case studies illustrated variations in manufacturing environments, including virtual manufacturing, by-products, authorized recipes, cut-to-size material, and the use of engineering versus production bills of material.

Chapter 4

Sales and
Operations Planning

A firm's sales and operations planning (S&OP) process starts with the definition of all demands for the firm's goods and services. It formulates *game plans* that drive supply chain activities to meet those demands. Hence, an effective S&OP game plan requires consideration of both demands and supplies. The nature of each product's game plan depends on the environment. The game plan may focus on stocked end-items in distribution and make-to-stock manufacturing environments. The game plan for a make-to-order manufactured product depends on the level of stocked components and the need for direct linkage between production orders and sales orders. The game plan for a multisite environment may require consideration of inventory replenishment across a distribution network. Variations in production capabilities such as lean manufacturing also affect the game plan. The saleable products for many firms represent a mixture of environments.

Independent demands provide the logical starting point for formulating an S&OP game plan. The logic underlying planning calculations and demand-pull philosophies is built on chasing demands. Independent demands consist of sales orders or forecasts or a combination of both.

Since the nature of an item's S&OP game plan depends on the environment, several common scenarios are used to illustrate considerations about demand and how to formulate a game plan. The scenarios included here represent single-site environments involved in distribution and manufacturing; Chapter 9 provides additional scenarios involving multisite operations.

An effective S&OP game plan results in fewer stock-outs, shorter delivery lead-times, higher on-time shipping percentages, a manageable amount of expediting, and improved customer service. Several guidelines are suggested to improve a firm's sales and operations planning process and the effectiveness of each product's game plan.

Identifying Demands

Sales orders identify actual demands. Actual demands may drive all supply chain activities when the sales orders with future ship dates exceed the cumulative lead-time to obtain and ship a product. However, actual demands must be anticipated when selling a product from inventory. One approach to stocking products in advance of sales orders involves a sales forecast, and the combination of sales forecast and sales orders defines demand for the saleable item. A second approach involves an order-point replenishment method, where the reorder point represents forecasted demand over the item's lead-time.

A make-to-order manufactured item may be built from stocked components. One approach to stocking components in advance of sales orders involves a component forecast, and the combination of component forecast and dependent demand defines demand for the component. A second approach involves an order-point replenishment method.

Sales Order Demand

A sales order line defines an actual demand for an item, expressed as a quantity, date, and ship-from location. A blanket sales order line also defines an actual demand for an item and location. Sales orders linked to the blanket order line consume the blanket order quantity. In this sense, a blanket sales order represents a forecast by customer.

Sales Forecast Demand

A sales forecast defines an estimated demand for a stocked item, expressed as a quantity, date, and ship-from location. Each sales forecast represents the desired inventory level on the specified date. Planning logic considers the combination of sales orders and forecasts in calculating requirements. Sales orders consume the sales forecast to avoid doubled-up requirements. This is termed *forecast consumption logic*. Forecast consumption logic reflects an implied forecast period defined by the sales forecast dates. An example may help. When an item's sales forecasts are defined on the first of each month, for example, a sales order consumes forecast within a given month based on the ship date. Unconsumed forecast rolls forward throughout the implied forecast period of a month, and gets ignored when the system work date matches or exceeds the next forecast date. The same logic applies to other implied forecast periods, such as sales forecasts entered with weekly or intermittent dates.

Multiple sets of sales forecast data can be defined, where each set is uniquely identified by a user-defined name. Each set may contain sales forecast data and component forecast data (described below) by location, so that each set is termed a *production forecast*. Planning calculations only use the set of forecast data identified on the manufacturing setup screen. Multiple sets of forecast data often reflect various scenarios for simulation purposes, or forecast revisions based on changing market conditions. A set of forecast data can be copied to a new set and subsequently revised. This approach supports comparison of actual demand to a selected set of forecasted demand.

Statistical Forecasting and Demand Planning

Forecasted demands can be based on many factors, such as management intuition, the current pipeline of prospects and quotes, and sales history. An item's sales history—typically reflecting posted shipments or item ledger entries about shipments—provides the basis for generating a statistical forecast in weekly or monthly increments. A sales forecast by location can be based on the best fit of various forecasting techniques. Projected quantities can be optionally overridden, and then used to automatically update a set of sales forecast data for use by planning calculations.

Component Forecast Demand

A component forecast defines an estimated demand for a stocked component, expressed as a quantity, date, and location. A component forecast is different from a sales forecast. A sales order for an end-item does not consume component forecast, so that a different type of forecast consumption logic must be used to avoid doubled-up requirements. In this case, the creation of a purchase order, production order, transfer order, or system-suggested order for the item consumes an item's component forecast. The system uses an implied forecast period defined by the component forecast dates. The order's scheduled receipt date acts as the basis for consuming component forecast. The unconsumed component forecast rolls forward throughout the implied forecast period, and is ignored when the system work date matches or exceeds the next forecast date.

Anticipating Demand Using Order-Point Logic

An order-point replenishment method provides an alternative to forecasts when anticipating demand for a location's stocked material. Time-phased order-point logic suggests replenishment when an SKU's projected available balance falls below its reorder point. The reorder point quantity represents estimated demand over the SKU's lead-time. This means planning calculations suggest an SKU's replenishment orders based on sales orders with future shipment dates. A time-phased order point approach does not require forecasted demand, but forecasts, if entered, will be considered by planning calculations.

Anticipating Demand Variations Using an Inventory Plan

Many firms carry additional inventory to anticipate variations in customer demand and meet customer service objectives regarding stockouts, partial shipments, and delivery lead-times. The additional inventory is termed an *inventory plan*. An inventory plan is typically expressed for SKUs at the highest possible stocking level, such as saleable end-items that are purchased or manufactured to stock. A make-to-order manufacturer, on the other hand, typically expresses an inventory plan for stocked components.

An inventory plan can be explicitly expressed as an SKU's safety stock quantity or as a safety lead-time. The safety lead-time represents a buffer against delayed receipts, but it also represents a type of inventory plan.

An implicit inventory plan can be expressed in several different ways. With an order-point replenishment method, the extent to which a reorder point exceeds typical demand over lead-time represents an implicit inventory plan. Suggested order quantities represent an implicit inventory plan when they exceed typical demand over the reorder cycle, or when inflated by order modifiers. The order modifiers and reorder cycle provide a similar implicit inventory plan for a replenishment method based on MRP logic.

Other Sources of Demand

Visibility of all demands is critical to formulating an effective S&OP game plan. Surprise demands can cause shortages that impact customer service or production and result in expediting. Some sources of demand may need interpretation or alternative ways to express the demand, as illustrated in the following examples.

Customer Schedules   Customer schedules represent a combination of sales orders (in the near term) and forecasts (in the longer term), and often require time-frame policies for proper interpretation. A blanket sales order provides one approach for defining a customer schedule, with sales orders representing releases within the customer schedule.

Internal Sales Orders   An internal sales order may be required to initiate production and/or procurement activities prior to obtaining the customer's purchase order. Once obtained, the designated customer can be changed on the sales order.

Customer Service Demands   Customer service may require material for loaners, exhibition items, donations, replacement items, and repairs.

Field Service Demands   Field service may require spare parts for selling to customers, and for repair and field service projects.

Engineering Prototypes   Prototypes may be built for internal or external customers, with requirements for material and production capacity. Procurement and production activity may also be initiated on new products with partially defined bills.

Quality   Quality often requires validation lots or first articles, especially during ramp-up to production lot sizes. Other quality-related demands can be embedded in planned manufacturing scrap, so that planning calculations identify the additional requirements for material and capacity.

Common Scenarios for Sales and Operations Planning

The nature of an S&OP game plan depends on several factors, such as the need to anticipate demand and the item's primary source of supply. Consideration of these factors can be illustrated with four common scenarios. The first two scenarios reflect stocked end-items, while the next two scenarios reflect make-to-order manufactured products. Replenishment of stocked material could be based on forecasted demand or order point logic, but the following explanations focus on the use of forecasted demand.

Scenario #1: Stocked End-Items in a Distribution Environment

Most distribution environments carry inventory of purchased items in anticipation of actual demand. As shown in Figure 4.1, demands consist of sales orders and sales forecasts by location. Sales orders consume sales forecast and drive shipping activities, and the combination of forecasts and sales orders drives the item's master schedule comprised of purchase orders.

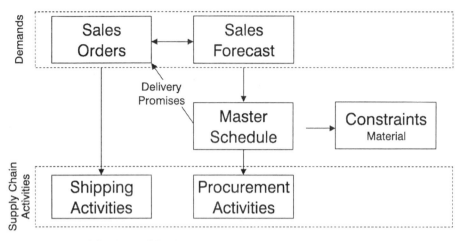

Figure 4.1   S&OP for a Distribution Item

Procurement activities are driven by existing purchase orders and by suggested new purchases. Planning calculations help formulate a realistic game plan by identifying potential material constraints on a requisition worksheet. An unrealistic rescheduling suggestion is identified by a due date earlier than today's date. Another unrealistic suggestion involves an expedited purchase inside normal lead-time, identified by an order start date earlier than today's date.

Unrealistic situations in the supply chain often require changes to sales orders. An analysis of an item's supplies and demands may be required to understand a situation and make the appropriate decision. Typical analysis tools include a time-phased summary of an item's supplies and demands (such as the *Item Availability by Period* window) and a drill-down to specific supplies and demands.

The ability to make realistic delivery promises on sales orders helps ensure a realistic game plan and avoids excessive expediting. Order promises identify the earliest ship date for a specified quantity and location. Order promises based on available-to-promise (ATP) logic consider inventory and scheduled receipts, whereas capable-to-promise (CTP) logic considers the item's lead-time for out-of-stock conditions.

Scenario #2: S&OP for a Make-to-Stock Manufactured Product

The S&OP approach for a make-to-stock manufactured product is almost exactly the same as a distribution item, since it requires inventory to anticipate

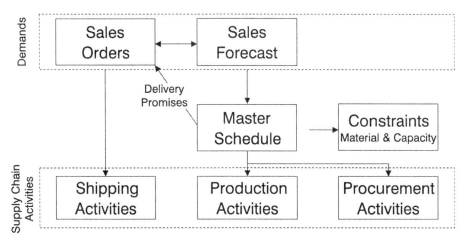

Figure 4.2 S&OP for a MTS Manufactured Item

actual demand. As shown in Figure 4.2, demands consist of sales orders and sales forecasts by location. Sales orders consume sales forecast and drive shipping activities, and the combination of forecasts and sales orders drives the item's master schedule comprised of production orders.

Production and procurement activities are driven by existing production orders and by suggestions for new production orders. Planning calculations help formulate a realistic game plan by identifying potential material and capacity constraints. A planning worksheet identifies potential material constraints related to the end-item and its manufactured and purchased components. The worksheet indicates an unrealistic rescheduling suggestion when the due date is earlier than today's date. Another unrealistic suggestion may involve an expedited purchase inside normal lead-time, identified by an order start date earlier than today's date.

Work center load analysis identifies potential capacity constraints in terms of overloaded periods. In overloaded periods, adjustments to available capacity (such as overtime and personnel transfers) or adjustments to loads (such as alternate operations) can help overcome the capacity constraint.

Unrealistic situations in the supply chain often require changes to the master schedule or to sales orders. An analysis of an item's supplies and demands may be required to understand a situation and make the appropriate decision. Typical analysis tools include a time-phased summary of an item's supplies and demands, and a drill-down to specific supplies and demands.

The ability to make realistic delivery promises on sales orders helps ensure a realistic game plan and avoids excessive expediting. Order promises identify the earliest ship date for a specified quantity and location, using either available-to-promise (ATP) logic or capable-to-promise (CTP) logic.

Use of a Manually Maintained Master Schedule for Stocked Items

Some manufacturers use a manually maintained master schedule for stocked items. Firm and released production orders define the master schedule. A manual reordering policy means that planning calculations do not suggest changes to the master schedule. The manually maintained master schedule reflects the planner's decision-making logic about how to meet demands, therefore eliminating the need for entering forecasted demand and inventory plans.

Scenario #3: S&OP for a Completely Make-to-Order Product

The S&OP approach for a completely make-to-order product focuses on sales orders, often preceded by a sales quote. For sales orders, a projected shipment date can be calculated using capable-to-promise logic when the product's bills and routings have been defined. In some cases, information about the product's bills and routing may not be completely defined at the time of sales order placement, or the definition evolves over time. One approach to handling sales orders for these partially defined products builds on the use of master bills, as described below in the breakout box concerning S&OP for partially defined make-to-order products.

In other cases, the make-to-order product represents a one-time demand for a yet-to-be-designed custom product. One approach to handling a custom product configuration builds on the use of order-dependent bills (rather than master bills). The configuration is often defined before entry of a sales order. Chapter 8 summarizes how to use a simulated production order for a one-time custom product, convert or copy it to a production order, and calculate a projected completion date based on CTP logic

Production orders for each make-to-order product typically have direct linkage to the sales order. A make-to-order environment can optionally use production orders indirectly linked to sales orders. Planning calculations coordinate production and procurement activities to ship the sales orders on time. The planning calculations identify potential material and capacity constraints on a planning worksheet and work center load analysis, as described in the previous scenario.

S&OP for Partially Defined Make-to-Order Products

The definition of a product's bills and routing may be incomplete at the time of sales order placement. An incomplete design may reflect several conditions, such as rough quotes, evolving customer specifications, or requirements for further engineering design to specify part numbers and drawings. In many cases, procurement and production activities must be initiated for critical-path components before the design has been completed.

Planning calculations can use partially defined bills and routings to help coordinate these supply chain activities. Several suggestions may help. First, basic decisions must be made about using master bills or order-dependent bills to define product structure, and about the need for identifying intermediate subassemblies. Further discussion assumes use of the master bills.

The next steps involve defining items for critical-path components, such as key subassemblies and long lead-time purchased material, so that orders can be initiated. A critical-path manufactured item requires additional information about its bill of material. The master bills must have a certified status even if they are partially defined. In this way, planning calculations can generate suggested action messages based on the evolving definition of product structure.

Scenario #4: Make-to-Order Product Built from Stocked Components

The S&OP approach for a partially make-to-order product requires component inventory in anticipation of actual demand. The level of stocked components must reflect the desired delivery lead-time with respect to the item's product structure. For example, components stocked at the first level provide the shortest delivery lead-time. A stocked component may reflect other considerations, such as intermittent delivery or some production or purchasing constraint.

As shown in Figure 4.3, independent demands consist of end-item sales orders and component forecasts by location. Component forecasts drive the master schedules for stocked material, whereas sales orders drive the finishing schedules (also called *final assembly schedules*) for the end-item and any make-to-order components.

Order promises identify the earliest ship date for a specified quantity using CTP logic. Planning calculations coordinate production and procurement activities to replenish stocked components and meet sales order requirements. The planning calculations identify potential material and capacity constraints on a planning worksheet and work center load analysis, as described in a previous scenario.

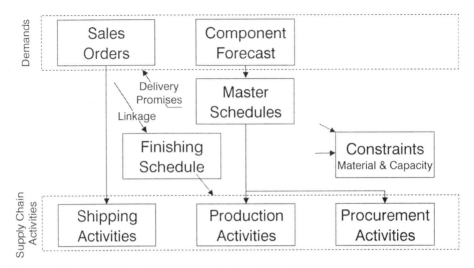

Figure 4.3   S&OP for a MTO Manufactured Product

Guidelines Concerning S&OP Game Plans

Effective game plans lead to improved firm performance and bottom-line results. Metrics include reductions in stock-outs, delivery lead-time, missed shipments, partial shipments, and expediting efforts, and improvements in customer service. The lack of effective game plans is typically cited as a leading cause of poor system implementation. The following guidelines provide suggestions for improving the effectiveness of S&OP game plans.

Minimum Planning Horizon for Each Game Plan   A saleable item's cumulative lead-time represents the minimum horizon for a game plan.

Reviewing and Updating Game Plans   The process for reviewing and updating each game plan should be embedded into the firm's regularly scheduled management meetings focusing on demands and supply chain activities. An agreed-upon game plan reflects a balance of conflicting objectives related to various functional areas, such as sales, engineering, manufacturing, purchasing, and accounting.

Primary Responsibility for Maintaining Game Plans   The person(s) acting as a master scheduler maintains the game plans and obtains management agreement. This role typically requires an in-depth understanding of sales and supply chain capabilities, as well as the political power to achieve agreed-upon game plans. The responsibility for providing sales order and forecast data typically belongs to the sales function, with a hand-off to the master scheduler.

Formulating Realistic Game Plans Realistic game plans require identification of capacity and material exceptions that would constrain the plans, and then eliminating the constraints or changing the plan. Identification of material-related exceptions typically starts with suggested actions on a planning worksheet, while capacity exceptions are identified using work center load analysis. In many cases, a realistic game plan must anticipate demands and demand variations via forecasts and inventory plans for stocked material.

Enforcing Near-Term Schedule Stability Near-term schedule stability provides one solution for resolving many conflicting objectives, such as improving competitive efficiencies in purchasing and production and reducing exceptions requiring expediting. It provides a stable target for coordinating supply chain activities and removes most alibis for missed schedules. Near-term schedule stability can benefit from inventory plans and realistic order promises about shipment dates. It involves a basic trade-off with objectives requiring fast response time and frequent schedule changes. The critical issue is that management recognizes the trade-offs to minimize near-term changes.

Making Realistic Sales Order Promises Realistic delivery promises represent the key link between sales commitments and supply chain activities. Delivery promises can be based on an item's existing inventory and scheduled receipts (via ATP logic), or on lead-times to purchase and/or manufacture the item (via CTP logic). The critical issue is to reduce and isolate the number of sales order exceptions requiring expediting. One solution approach involves splitting delivery across two sales order line items with different shipment dates.

Maintaining Valid Sales Order Shipment Dates Sales order shipment dates are used by planning calculations to communicate required supply chain activities. Changes in supply chain activities and/or demands sometimes require updates to indicate later shipment dates. In particular, past due shipment dates must be updated to reflect a current or future date.

Executing Supply Chain Activities to Plan Planning calculations make an underlying assumption that everyone works to plan, and the system provides coordination tools to communicate needed action. For example, it is assumed that procurement will ensure timely delivery of purchased material so that manufacturing can meet production schedules. It is assumed distribution will make on-time shipments because sales made valid delivery promises and procurement and production are working to plan. An unmanageable number of exceptions will impact this underlying assumption and the usefulness of coordination tools.

Reducing Exceptions Requiring Expediting The intent of near-term schedule stability, valid delivery promises and shipment dates, realistic game plans, and executing to plan is to reduce the number of exceptions to a manageable level. This improves the usefulness of coordination tools to meet the game plans.

Business Analytics and S&OP

The S&OP process translates business plans (expressed in dollars) into sales, production, and inventory plans (expressed in units), and requires management information about planned and actual results for each game plan. Business analytics—also termed business intelligence, data warehouses, and executive information systems—provides one way to present this management information in dollars and units. The data reflects summarized information with drill-down to more detail. The results are presented in a variety of formats—ranging from lists and tables to graphs and charts—for financial and operational metrics. For example, the set of sales forecast data provides the basis for planned sales while shipment history defines actual sales. Business analytics can also highlight key performance indicators about operational metrics, such as on-time shipping percentages, production performance (about quality, delivery, and costs) and vendor performance.

Case Studies

Case #17: S&OP Simulations Many firms require simulations to assess the impact of changing demands or supplies. Using multiple sets of forecast data to represent various scenarios, and a designated set of forecast data for planning calculation purposes, the management team can analyze the impact of changing demands on material and capacity requirements. The management team can also analyze the impact of using only sales order demand (and ignoring forecasted demand) by not designating a set of forecast data for planning calculation purposes.

**Case #18: Common Component Forecast for Process Manu-
facturing**   One product line within the Batch Process company consists
of many end-items built to order from a common manufactured item. The
bill of material for each end-item identifies the common manufactured item
and packaging components such as labels and bottles. In this case, the S&OP
game plans for packaging components are expressed in terms of min-max
quantities, while a component forecast drives production of the common
manufactured item.

**Case #19: Kanban Coordination in Consumer Products Man-
ufacturing**   The Consumer Products company recently implemented a
dedicated manufacturing cell for producing one product line. They wanted
minimal reporting requirements and automatic generation of Kanban cards to
coordinate production activities. Prior to cut-over for production in the new
manufacturing cell on July 1, they used component date effectivities in the
bills for each affected item to flatten the product structure. Routing information was only defined for the end-items, using a routing revision (with a July 1
start date) that defined run rates in the manufacturing cell. Purchased components were kept in floor stock bin locations with bin replenishment based on
projected daily usage rates and a min-max reordering policy. Based on
end-item demands and product structure information, planning calculations
were customized to calculate projected daily usage rates for components and
to generate Kanban cards for end-items and some intermediates. A customization provided an orderless approach to reporting end-item output. Only the
item number and a completed quantity were reported, which then triggered
auto-deduction of components from the floor stock bin locations.

Case #20: S&OP by Job for Construction Material   The Distribution company sold several product lines to the commercial construction
industry, where the products also required job-specific installation services.
Each job involved multiple phases and tasks (with material and resource requirements) that were closely tied to progress on the construction site. For example, multiple steps were required for plumbing and electrical installation.
Using the job functionality within Navision, and customizations to planning
calculations and a job schedule board, the time-phased requirements for material and resources were synchronized with scheduled installation dates at the
construction sites.

Case #21: Statistical Forecasting   The Distribution company used
statistical forecasting to calculate future sales demand in monthly increments
based on historical data. This required historical data about previous years

(prior to cutover to Microsoft Navision). In addition to shipments, the historical data included customer returns, credit memos, and selected inventory adjustments. Further refinements included the requested shipment date (to give a true picture of demand patterns) and information about sales of substitute items. Statistical forecast information was also needed to drive component forecasts for stocked components, where the historical data reflected item ledger entries about usage rather than shipments.

Case #22: Planning Bills for Make-to-Order Equipment.

The Equipment company wanted to perform sales forecasting using a planning bill that specified mix percentages for equipment options. Building on the standardized functionality for make-to-order manufactured items, they modified planning calculations so that a sales forecast demand blew through the product structure for a make-to-order item and created component forecast demand for stocked components. The planning bill was also used during order entry as the basis for selecting options in a configuration. A further modification ensured the system automatically created an order-dependent bill with the selected options when the user generated production orders from the sales order.[1] This approach resulted in matched sets of components, recognized planned changes in bills and routings, provided visibility of capacity requirements, and simplified the forecasting process (compared to entering individual component forecasts for stocked items).

Case #23: Manual Master Scheduling for Medical Devices

The Equipment company produced a line of medical devices that required a manually maintained master schedule to reflect the planner's decision-making logic about production constraints. The medical devices required an expensive outside operation for sterilizing a batch of multiple end-items. The scheduling considerations included a cost-benefit analysis about amortizing the fixed fee for sterilization over the largest possible batch weight subject to a batch weight maximum while still building the product mix for customer demands and avoiding excess inventory. A manual schedule proved most effective for this case.

Case #24: S&OP for a One-Time Product

The Fabricated Products company often designed and built a one-time product to customer specifications. They used a simulated production order and order-dependent bills to

---

[1] See *Maximizing Your ERP System* for further explanation of planning bills (pp. 151–156) and their use in forecasting (pp. 183–187).

define the product structure and to calculate estimated costs. This information was used to calculate a projected completion date based on forward scheduling logic. After receiving the sales order, this information was used to create a released production order and drive purchasing and production activities. Chapter 8 provides further explanation about using a simulated production for one-time products.

Executive Summary

The ability to run the company from the top requires a sales and operations planning (S&OP) process that formulates an S&OP game plan for each saleable product. The nature of each game plan depends on several factors such as the visibility of demands, delivery lead-time, and a make-to-stock versus make-to-order production strategy. The starting point for each game plan requires identification of all sources of demand such as sales orders and forecasts, and forecast consumption logic determines how the combination of these demands drive supply chain activities. Several scenarios illustrated how to formulate game plans for a distribution product and three types of manufactured products (make-to-stock, completely make-to-order, and partially make-to-order). Special cases involved a manually maintained master schedule and a partially defined make-to-order product. Guidelines were suggested to improve S&OP game plans, such as how to formulate realistic game plans, enforce near-term schedule stability, and make realistic delivery promises. The case studies highlighted variations in S&OP game plans, such as S&OP simulations, Kanban coordination, planning bills, statistical forecasting, and one-time products.

Chapter 5

Sales Order Processing

Sales orders capture demands for the firm's products and services. Sales orders comprise a key element in two larger contexts: the sales and operations (S&OP) game plan driving supply order management and customer service across the customer relationship life cycle. The sales order often represents one step in the customer relationship, and may involve collaborative work in the sales channel as well as the supply chain. Only a subset of customer information directly relates to sales order processing, while other customer information such as contacts relates to other steps in the customer relationship.

Distributors and manufacturers focus on sales orders for material items. These orders may originate from one or more order streams, such as direct customer communication with order entry personnel, telemarketing, sales representatives, Web-placed orders, and electronically transmitted customer schedules. Variations in sales orders can be expressed for individual line items. However, the basic structure of a sales order remains the same regardless of order stream and variation, and sales orders for material items provide the organizing focus for further explanation.

Customer Information

Each customer is defined in a customer master file by a unique identifier. Sold-to and bill-to customers require unique identifiers. The customer master file defines information for sales order processing and other purposes such as sales analysis and accounting. Several data elements have particular significance to sales order management

- ◆ *Ship-to Addresses.* A sold-to customer can have one or more ship-to addresses for shipment purposes. Additional shipping information can be defined for each ship-to address, such as the preferred ship-from site and the preferred shipping agent and service type. These values act as defaults in a sales order for the customer's ship-to address.

- *Bill-to Customer.* Each customer can optionally have a designated bill-to customer that acts as a default on sales orders, where the bill-to customer determines applicable pricing and discounts.

- *Attributes Related to Pricing and Discounts.* A customer price group and discount group can be used for defining item prices and discounts, respectively. Each customer can also have invoice discounts and service charges related to the total value of a sales order.

- *Attributes Related to G/L Account Number Assignment.* General ledger (G/L) account number assignment reflects the customer posting group and business posting group assigned to a customer. A customer posting group defines G/L account numbers such as receivables and service charges. A business posting group works in combination with an item's product posting group to define G/L account numbers such as sales, cost of sales, and discounts. These attributes also serve sales analysis purposes.

- *Analytic Dimensions for a Customer.* The analytic dimensions assigned to a customer provide a means to analyze sales by customer type. They can be used in conjunction with analytic dimensions assigned to other entities, such as items, sales campaigns, and sales people, to provide multidimensional sales analyses.

- *Customer Hold Status.* A customer hold status (termed a *blocked status*) can prevent all transactions from being recorded, or only prevent shipments or payments to the customer

- *Customer-Related Comments.* Comments are generally used for internal purposes, and can be defined with multiple lines of free-form text. Each line may be assigned a date and a user-defined code to sort and filter comments, such as comments related to accounting or sales.

- *Biztalk Partner Information.* The ability to exchange documents electronically requires identification of the customer as a Biztalk partner, the types of authorized documents, and rules for exchanging information. Outbound documents include sales order confirmations, shipment notifications, and sales quotes; inbound documents include sales orders and requests for a sales quote.

Summarized information about a customer can be viewed in several ways. A customer's statistics include month-to-date (MTD) and year-to-date (YTD) values for sales, profits, invoices, and payments. The total value of sales and profits can be viewed across time, such as monthly or quarterly time increments. Entry statistics for a customer include MTD and YTD transaction counts (such as the number of invoices, payments, and credit memos), as well as calculations for average collection period and largest balance. Transaction detail can also be viewed by type of sales document, such as outstanding quotes, sales orders, and return orders.

Sales Orders

Sales orders for material items define demands and drive supply chain activities. Variations of sales orders drive purchase orders for drop shipments and special orders, and production orders directly linked to a sales order. Sales order line items may be for other types of sales, such as selling resource time and special charges.

The structure of a sales order serves as the starting point for further explanation. This section covers variations in sales order processing and highlights key considerations such as order-related text, delivery promises, and material reservations.

Structure and Life Cycle of a Sales Order for Material Items

The basic structure of a sales order consists of header information and line item information, where the sales order number can be manually or automatically assigned. As a reflection of this basic structure, the sales order number and line number uniquely identify a scheduled shipment. The sales order header identifies the sold-to customer and the customer's ship-to address, and optionally identifies a different customer for bill-to purposes. This customer information provides default values for the sales order header, and some header information provides default values for the line items.

The life cycle of a sales order consists of several steps, with two steps represented by an order status as explained below.

- ◆ *Open.* An open status indicates the sales order is being created. An order header has been created, and one or more line items can be defined. Information can be changed on the sales order and an order acknowledgment printed, but the order cannot be shipped. The order status must be manually changed from open to released.

- ◆ *Released.* A released status indicates the sales order information has been completely entered and all line items are released for shipment. Information cannot be changed on a released sales order, but it can be manually reopened to allow changes. A released order allows shipment transactions and generation of pick documents for warehouse management purposes.

A line item is automatically flagged as completely shipped when its shipped quantity equals the order quantity. This represents an implied closure. The order is automatically deleted when order quantities for all line items have been posted as completely shipped and invoiced. Historical information about a system-deleted sales order can be viewed on the screens for posted shipments and posted credit memos. Prior to deletion, a sales order can be optionally archived for the purpose of historical look-up or comparison of archived versions.

Sales Order Variations for Material Items

Several variations in sales order line items can be designated for material items, such as drop shipments, special orders, and kit items. Production orders can also be generated for line items containing a manufactured item.

Special Order for Purchased Material   A line item can be designated as a special order, typically for a new non-stock item but also for an existing item or non-stock item. The item can be shipped after purchase order receipt.

Drop Shipment for Purchased Material   A line item can be designated as a drop shipment, with the ship-to address information specified in the sales order header. After creation of the associated purchase order, a purchase order receipt and then a sales order shipment and invoice must be entered, followed by entry of the purchase invoice.

Kit of Material Items   Kit items are defined on the item master along with an assembly list of components. The kit item can represent a product that is sold and priced as a single item or as a set of components. Hence, a kit item can appear as a single line item or multiple line items on a sales order.

Sales Order Linkage to Production Orders   Many make-to-order manufacturing environments require production orders linked to sales orders. Several approaches can be used to establish direct linkage between the sales order and production order(s). The production order can be generated from the sales order during order entry, manually entered afterward (with direct reference to the sales order), or generated by planning calculations for a make-to-order manufactured item. These methods were previously described in Chapter 3.

Other Types of Sales Order Line Items

A sales order for a material item represents one type of line item. Other line item types can be designated, such as text, resource time, item charges, G/L charges, and fixed asset.

* *Line Item Text.* Line item text can be manually entered as a description, or selected from a list of predefined standard text (identified by standard text codes). Multiple lines of line item text can be entered. The user can optionally override the predefined standard text description.

* *Selling Resource Time.* A resource item typically represents a person or machine, with information defined in a separate resource master. A resource item can be shipped and invoiced without requiring an inventory balance.

* *G/L Charges.* A sales order line specified for a G/L account can be shipped and invoiced without requiring an inventory balance. Typical examples include restocking charges, sales allowance, freight, setup fees, or other special charges that are not associated with any given item.

* *Item Charges.* A sales order line specified for item charges also represents a special charge (as described above), but in this case it must be assigned or allocated to one or more line items. An item charge code must be predefined and associated with relevant G/L account numbers such as sales and cost of sales. An example of the user-defined code would be "freight" or "setup fee." Item charges can be manually or automatically assigned to other line items, with automatic assignment based on equal amounts per line or proportional amounts based on value.

* *Selling a Fixed Asset.* The sales order line indicates the identifier for a fixed asset and the sales price, and the shipment transaction updates information in the fixed assets application.

Pricing and Discounting on Sales Orders

An item's price and discounts can be automatically or manually assigned on a sales order, as previously described in Chapter 2. Automatic assignment typically reflects a predefined price book or a negotiated agreement with the customer. The pricing and discounting information applies to individual sales order line items.

Some sales order situations require an invoice discount or service charge based on total order value. The amount can be manually assigned or automatically calculated. Automatic calculation reflects information defined for each customer, with invoice discounts expressed as a percentage and service charges expressed as an amount. For example, an order exceeding $100 obtains a 10 percent discount, or a $25 service charge applies to a minimum order value of less than $500. The service charge appears as a separate line on the sales order (identified by the G/L account description for service charges). An invoice discount percentage and a service charge amount can both be defined for a customer.

Sales Order Considerations

Sales order processing in a simplistic sense involves identification of the customer and the desired item, quantity, price, and ship-from location. Many situations require additional considerations, such as the use of textual explanations, customer item numbers, delivery promises, and so forth.

Order-Related Text   Many situations require textual explanations or additional descriptive information about the sales order and its line items. Order-related text can be specified in three ways: as comments in the order header, as line item text, and as extended text carried forward from the item master.

- *Comments.* An order-related comment can be defined with multiple lines of free-form text. Several policies determine whether comments will carry forward to related sales documents. For example, sales setup policies determine whether order-related comments will be carried forward from a blanket order, or whether order-related comments will be subsequently copied to the shipment and invoice.

- *Line Item Text.* Line item text can be manually entered as a description, or selected from a list of predefined standard text and optionally overridden.

- *Carry Forward of Item-Related Extended Text.* Extended text is defined for a specific item, along with effectivity dates and policies that determine whether it will carry forward to sales documents such as the sales order. An item's extended text can be automatically added to sales order line items (based on an item policy) or inserted upon manual request during order entry. The system considers the effectivity dates specified for the extended text. The extended text description can be overridden on the document.

Using Item Numbers vs. Cross-Reference Numbers   A sales order line item for material can identify the item number or a cross-reference number that represents the customer item number or a catalog number.

Shipment Dates and Delivery Dates   Each sales order line identifies three delivery dates: requested, promised, and planned delivery dates. The requested delivery date acts as reference information. Demands and shipments

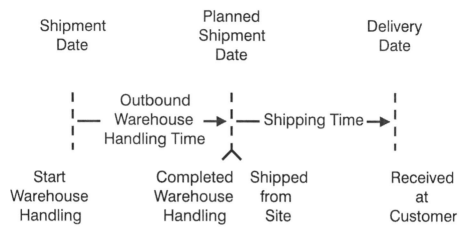

Figure 5.1   Sales Order Delivery Dates vs. Shipment Dates

are driven by the promised delivery date, or by the planned delivery date when a promised date has not been specified. The promised and requested delivery dates specified in the order header act as default values for each line item; they also provide a means for mass updating all line item delivery dates. These delivery dates provide the basis for measuring on-time shipments.

Each sales order line item also identifies two shipment dates that represent the start and completion of outbound warehouse handling activities such as picking, packing, and labeling an order's items. These dates are termed the *shipment date* and *planned shipment date*, as shown in Figure 5.1. Each ship-from location has a specified outbound warehouse handling time, such as one working day, which defaults to the line item.

The difference between a planned shipment date and delivery date represents the shipping time for transporting materials between the ship-from site and the customer's ship-to location. The system assigns a shipping time that reflects the shipping agent and service (such as FedEx second-day delivery) specified for the line item. This line item information defaults from the header, which defaults from the customer ship-to address. Figure 5.1 illustrates the differences between shipment dates and delivery dates.

Making Delivery Promises   Order promises identify the earliest ship date for a specified quantity of a material item. Order promises based on available-to-promise (ATP) logic consider the item's inventory and scheduled receipts, and gross requirements such as other sales order commitments. In contrast, order promises based on capable-to-promise (CTP) logic consider the item's lead-time as previously described in Chapters 2 and 3.

The order promising function can be invoked during entry of a sales order. It applies to all line items on the sales order, using either ATP logic or CTP logic or both. The user can accept the calculations for earliest ship dates, and the system automatically updates all sales order line items. A company setup policy defines a look-ahead window (such as 30 or 90 days) for ATP purposes; an inventory setup policy defines a delay (such as 1 or 2 days) before the lead-time associated with a new order can be considered for CTP purposes.

Identifying Past Due Shipment Dates The system automatically flags sales order line items as *late order shipping* when the work date exceeds the shipment date.

Aligning Shipment Dates on Sales Order Lines An open sales order allows changes to planned shipment dates, either on an individual line item basis or via mass change.

+ *Changes to Individual line Items.* A change to the planned shipment date (or delivery date) indicates when a line item will really ship, regardless of promises or customer requests. However, the planned shipment date is automatically realigned when the promised delivery date is changed.
+ *Mass Changes to All Line Items.* Changing the promised delivery date in the header can optionally realign all line items to the new date. An alternative approach can be used to align all lines to the latest shipment date assigned to a line.

Indicating a Special Order or Drop Shipment A purchasing code (defined as part of purchasing setup) indicates whether the line item is a special order or a drop-shipment.

Generating a Production Order for the Sales Order The create production order function provides options for selecting order status (planned, firm planned, or released) and order source (item or sales order), and then generates a production order linked to the sales order.

Reserving Material for a Sales Order A reservation (also termed a hard allocation) for an item's inventory can be made manually or automatically, subject to reservation policies defined for the item and customer. With manual assignment during order entry, the user can prompt a review of existing inventory and manually select inventory to be reserved. A production order or purchase order can also be reserved for a sales order. Reservations can be made for lot- and serial- traced material as well as non-traced material.

Stock-Out Warnings   An optional stock-out warning during the entry of a sales order line item identifies when there is insufficient available inventory at the ship-from site. It also indicates the earliest available date (based on the item's lead-time) and whether item substitutes exist. It does not provide time-phased available-to-promise information, and represents a simplistic tool for making valid delivery promises.

Identifying Item Substitutions for Sales Orders   A flag indicates whether substitute items exist for the item after entering line item data. Information about the substitute items (such as interchangeability, explanatory conditions, and availability) can be viewed, and selection of a substitute item automatically updates information on the sales order line item.

Generating a Credit Memo or Return Order from a Sales Order   Some situations require identification of items that must be returned or credited while a user is in the midst of sales order entry. These items can be identified as sales order line items with a negative quantity. The user can then choose whether to create a return order or a credit memo for the designated line items, and the designated lines are deleted from the sales order.

Using a Template to Create Line Items   A short-cut approach for creating multiple line items involves a template (termed a *standard customer sales code*). A template typically represents repeat orders although it may serve other creative purposes, such as viewing a group of related items for up-selling or cross-selling purposes. Another example includes a group of service parts that should be sold together. Each template has a user-defined identifier and defines a list of items and quantities. A template must be assigned to an individual customer before usage. A template can be viewed and selected during order entry, where selection automatically creates additional sales order line items for the template's items and quantities. Templates can also be created on the fly during order entry.

Creating a Sales Order via Copying an Existing Sales Document   The copy feature can be used to create sales order line items or the entire order from an existing sales document, such as another sales order, quote, or a previously shipped order. When copying just the line items, the system incrementally adds new line items with the same item, quantity, and ship-from site, and optionally recalculates prices and discounts based on the customer and date. The incremental additions allow multiple copy efforts. The system assigns a shipment date based on header information.

When copying an entire sales document, the system replaces the sales order header information (such as the customer) and deletes existing lines before copying the new lines.

Changing the Sell-to Customer on a Sales Order   Changing the sell-to customer for a sales order (prior to ledger entries) has several impacts. The change results in new header information and an optional change for the bill-to customer. Any existing line items get deleted and re-added with the applicable price and discount information, and the default ship-from site associated with the customer.

Sales Forecast Consumption by Sales Orders   A sales order line for a material item consumes the item's sales forecast (if specified). Forecast consumption logic considers the shipment date within an implied forecast period. Note that a sales order related to a blanket order consumes the blanket order quantity rather than a sales forecast.

Identifying Salespeople and Handling Commissions   The salesperson assigned to each customer acts as a default on sales orders for the bill-to customer, where salespeople (and their commission percentage) must be predefined. Sales commissions are calculated based on posted invoices and displayed on a Sales Commission Report.

Sending a Sales Order Confirmation   A sales order confirmation can be printed or faxed, printed to file and attached to an e-mail message, or sent via a Biztalk outbound document. An agreement concerning the Biztalk outbound document must be previously defined for the customer as part of the setup information for Biztalk partners; the system provides a warning when an agreement does not exist.

Statistics for Sales Orders   An order's statistics include calculated totals for sales, cost, and the profit amount and percentage, a calculated invoice discount that can be manually overridden, and calculated totals for quantity, volume, net weight, and gross weight. The statistics window also displays calculated tax amounts segmented by tax identifier.

Posting a Sales Order Shipment and Invoice

Shipping activities represent the completion of sales order processing, and different approaches can be taken to report shipping activity for material items. The basic approach focuses on reporting shipping activity against line items on an individual sales order. In many cases, the printed sales order serves as a pick list and turnaround document for recording actual quantities shipped from stocking locations. The turnaround document serves as the basis for entering data on the sales order window (or an equivalent version for shipping purposes) for all line items. The window displays default values for each line item's quantity and stocking location to help minimize data entry efforts. Posting the data creates a shipment and updates inventory balances. Some situations require an invoice to accompany the shipment, so that posting can optionally create the sales invoice. After posting a shipment, a Biztalk shipment notification can be generated from the posted shipment window.

Chapter 7 describes other approaches to reporting sales order shipments, such as using a pick document and shipment document.

Some customers want a single invoice for multiple shipments, as designated by the Combine Shipments flag on the customer master (which defaults to the sales order header). After shipments have been recorded, performing the periodic activity for Combine Shipments (for a selected sell-to or bill-to customer) gathers all the uninvoiced shipments into one invoice and optionally posts the invoices.

Other Types of Sales Documents and Methods for Creating a Sales Order

A sales quote, blanket sales order, and return order represent other types of sales documents, and provide an alternative method for creating a sales order. A sales order can also be created by an inbound Biztalk sales order transaction.

Sales Quotes

A sales quote specifies the item, quantity and UM, sales price, and planned shipment date for one or more line items, and acts like a sales order in many ways. For example, it uses the same approaches for pricing and discounting, cross reference identifiers, item substitutions, copy document, order-related text, and statistics. However, a quote cannot use order promising logic or reservations. A sales quote can be defined for an existing customer or a contact. A contact can be created on the fly, and a new customer can be created on the fly from the contact information.

A sales quote can be converted or copied to a sales order. When converting a quote, the system automatically assigns a separate sales order number, creates the same line items as the quote, and deletes the quote. Copying the quote allows multiple usage of the quotation.

An inbound Biztalk document can identify a request for sales quote. This information provides the basis for creating a sales quote that can be reviewed and modified, and then sent back to the customer as accepted or rejected. The inbound document identifies the line items to be quoted, such as the item, quantity, and UM. The rules for exchanging information determine whether the inbound requests should be manually accepted or used to automatically create a sales quote. In either case, a designated user can be notified via e-mail upon receipt of an inbound Biztalk request for sales quote.

A sales quote can be printed or faxed, printed to file and attached to an e-mail, or sent via a Biztalk outbound document. An agreement concerning the outbound document must be previously defined for the customer as part of the setup information for Biztalk partners.

Blanket Sales Orders

A blanket sales order specifies the item price and aggregate quantity for one or more line items, where each line item's aggregate quantity provides the basis for pricing and line discounts. Each sales order line item related to a blanket order inherits the item price and consumes the aggregate quantity. The cumulative sales order quantities cannot exceed the aggregate quantity.

Each line item on a blanket order also specifies a shipment date that represents an approximation of when the aggregate quantity will be shipped. Planning calculations treat a blanket order as a demand that reflects the specified shipment date and the unconsumed aggregate quantity. In this sense, a blanket sales order represents a sales forecast by customer that is consumed by related sales orders. The related sales orders do not consume an item's sales forecast.

The user can convert a blanket sales order into a sales order, based on a user-specified quantity (termed the *quantity to ship*) for applicable line items. This is sometimes referred to as a *release against the blanket sales order*. The system automatically assigns a separate sales order number, and identifies the originating blanket sales order and line number on each sales order line item. An alternative approach involves manual identification of the blanket sales order on a sales order line item. In either case, the system tracks the cumulative quantity shipped and invoiced for the blanket sales order.

The statistics for a blanket sales order include calculated totals for sales, cost, and the profit amount and percentage, calculated totals for quantity, volume, net weight, and gross weight, and calculated tax amounts segmented by tax identifier. The same statistics are also summarized for posted shipments and invoices related to the blanket sales order. The blanket sales order window provides access to detailed information about related transactions, such as shipments, invoices, returns, and credit memos.

Return Orders for Handling Customer Returns

A return order has a unique identifier that represents the return authorization number. A return order specifies a customer and bill-to-customer, and one or more line items. Each line item identifies an item, quantity and UM, price, ship-to location, and planned delivery date. A lot and serial number can be preassigned to incoming material (reflecting item tracking policies). The user can optionally designate return reason codes and the applicable document such as a posted invoice. A printed return order provides a return authorization document.

The process of handling customer returns can vary significantly depending on the circumstances. A simple process, for example, involves creating a return order for specified items and quantities, receiving the returned goods, and posting the receipt to update inventory balances and create a credit memo. This simple process provides the foundation for additional steps. For example, after creation of the return order, the user can optionally create return-related documents such as a new sales order for sending the same items as a replacement. Sending a different item as a replacement requires additional steps to add a line item to the return order (with a negative quantity) and then generate a sales order for sending the replacement item. For purchased items being returned from the customer, the user can optionally create a new purchase return order (for returning the customer's returned goods to the responsible vendor), and/or a new purchase order (for getting replacement items from the vendor). These examples illustrate a few of the variations in handling customer returns.

Creating a Sales Order from a Biztalk Inbound Document

An inbound Biztalk sales order document can be used for creating a sales order, with a designated user notified via e-mail upon document receipt. The inbound transaction must be previously authorized for the customer as part of the setup information for Biztalk partners. The inbound document contains sales order header information such as the sold-to and bill-to customer, as well as line item information about the item, quantity and UM, and ship-from site. Each line item also contains the price and discount information reflecting the customer agreements. The Biztalk partner setup information defines several rules for exchanging information:

- *Basis for Item Identification.* The rule determines whether the customer's transactions identify the internal item number or the common item number.

- *Manually Accept vs. Automatically Create the Sales Order.* Manual acceptance requires a review of the pending inbound sales orders and a decision to accept or reject each sales order.
- *Convert a Previous Quote to a Sales Order.* The referenced sales quote gets deleted and replaced with the sales order information.

Sales Analysis

Requirements for sales analysis information vary significantly between firms and decision makers within a firm. The system provides a number of standard sales analysis windows and reports, as illustrated below. Each company tends to develop customized reports to meet their unique requirements.

Sales Analysis for Individual Quotes and Orders
The statistics for an order or quote include calculated totals for sales, cost, and the profit amount and percentage.

Sales Analysis for Individual Customers
A customer's statistics include month-to-date (MTD) and year-to-date (YTD) values for sales, profits, invoices, and payments. The total value of sales and profits can be viewed across time, such as monthly or quarterly time increments. The Customer Sales Statistics report provides similar information for all customers. The Top Customers report identifies the largest customers in terms of revenue (or balance) over a specified time period

Sales Analysis for Individual Salespeople
The Salesperson Commission report provides summarized data and invoice detail about sales and profit (plus calculated commissions) for a specified date range. The Salesperson Statistics by Invoice report provides a breakdown of sales and actual margins after discounts. The statistics window for a salesperson displays the number of opportunities and the total and average value of opportunities.

Sales Analysis for Individual Items
The statistics window for an item displays sales, cost of sales, and profitability in total and in time increments such as monthly or quarterly. The analysis can reflect one or all locations, a specified date range, and per unit calculations (rather than totals). The window provides drill-down to specific invoices comprising the summarized values. Similar information is displayed for all items on the Item Sales Statistics report. The Sales History report identifies, for each item, the units sold, revenue, and profits by time period (such as monthly) over a specified date range.

Sales Analysis by Customer and Item   The Customer/Item Statistics report summarizes the units, revenue, and contribution margin for items sold to each customer over a specified date range. The same customer and item information can also be viewed by salesperson.

Sales Analysis by Dimension   This window provides a matrix view of summarized data tied to the analytical dimensions for customers, products, and other items. For example, it provides sales analysis by customer group across multiple time periods, or sales analysis by customer group and product group. The displayed values can reflect actual or budget amounts, or the variance.

Business Analytics and Sales Analysis

Sales analysis often requires summarized data for large volumes of detailed transaction data. Business analytics supports this data summarization with periodic data extractions into a data warehouse. With a packaged solution (such as targit.com), business analytics and the data warehouse offer an installation wizard and population tools to support out-of-the-box functionality with minimal technical expertise and implementation effort (such as one day). The cubes within the data warehouse can reflect several business areas, including customer, sales, inventory, vendor, purchase, and general ledger information. They can also reflect the analytical dimensions employed within Microsoft Navision, with predefined reports and *ad hoc* customized reports—presented as graphs, maps, charts, and objects.

Case Studies

Case #25: Automotive Parts Supplier and Customer Schedules   Production at an automotive parts supplier was driven by customer schedules updated weekly. The customer schedules provided authorization (termed releases) for shipping items and quantities on specified dates in the near-term horizon. They also provided projected requirements over the longer-term horizon. The customer required tracking of cumulative quantities. The customer schedules were defined as line items on a blanket sales order, with sales orders created by releases against the blanket order (with tracking of cumulative quantities shipped). The customer also required electronic shipment notification that was provided by a Biztalk document.

Case #26: Merging Customer Information   The merging of two customer accounts, typically stemming from acquisitions or customer duplicates, requires merging of all current and historical transactions to a new or existing customer. After the merge process, the balances, reports, and drill-downs treat the altered information as if it had been posted correctly from the beginning. Similar capabilities also apply to merging information about two vendors, items, and general ledger accounts.[1]

Case #27: Reserved Material in a Lot-Trace Environment
The Batch Process company produced lot-traced items with lot attributes that affected usage suitability. Each customer specified acceptable values for these lot attributes during sales order entry, and the applicable lots were reserved. Customizations helped to automate this business process. First, lot attributes were defined by product category and each item was assigned a product category. Second, attribute values were assigned to lot numbers of saleable end-items. Third, a profile of acceptable values for these lot attributes could be defined during sales order entry. Finally, the available-to-promise calculations were customized to identify existing lots with applicable lot values, and to optionally reserve the material for the sales order.

Case #28: Mobile Order Entry via Hand-Held Devices   The Consumer Products company had field sales representatives that wrote orders on paper forms that were faxed to the home office for manual rekeying. This manual system was replaced with hand-held devices (with a built in bar-code scanner) that allowed salespeople to enter quotes, orders, and invoices, and print them via a portable printer. At headquarters, the sales documents were seamlessly and automatically posted into Navision during each user's synchronization. The solution increased order efficiency and reduced errors, and allowed the average order size to grow significantly.

Case #29: Rules-Based Configurator for Equipment Manufacturer   The Equipment company offered numerous options and features for several models of equipment, and wanted a simple method for configuring products that would minimize time, errors, and engineering design assistance. To solve their requirements, they implemented a rules-based configurator software package tightly integrated with Navision functionality. The package supported user-defined questions and responses tailored to the customer's perception of the equipment applications, with a mapping between responses

---

[1] See www.CRGroup.com for additional information about the merge capabilities.

and the required bill of materials and routing operations for producing the configuration. The configurator enforced engineering design rules, calculated estimated costs, and also provided pricing based on responses and selected options.[2]

Case #30: Smart Part Numbers for Configurations
The Equipment company wanted to use a smart part number to identify the selected base unit and options, but did not want to create an item number for every possible combination of values. They also wanted to price, ship, and invoice a single line item. Using a rules-based configurator package (see Case #29) during sales order processing, the entry of a smart part number was automatically translated into the appropriate order-dependent bills (and routings) for production orders directly linked to the sales order line item. The production order description communicated the smart part number for manufacturing purposes.

Executive Summary

Sales orders capture demands for the firm's products and services, and comprise a key element in the larger contexts of customer relationship management and the S&OP process. In addition to sales orders for stocked material, sales order variations include drop shipments, special orders, kit items, and make-to-order manufactured items. Sales order considerations include order-related text, making delivery promises, reserving material, and item substitutions. Other types of sales documents include sales quotes, blanket sales orders, and sales returns; these can be used to create a sales order. A Biztalk document can also create a sales order. Sales analysis provides critical management information, and multidimensional analysis can be based on customer, product, salesperson, campaign, area, and other factors. The case studies highlight variations in sales order processing, including customer schedules, mobile order entry, and rules-based product configurators.

---

[2] See www.Foqus-ict.com\econ for additional information about a rules-based configurator.

Chapter 6

Purchase Order Processing

A primary responsibility of procurement is to coordinate and execute the supply chain activities driven by the firm's S&OP (sales and operations planning) game plans. Purchased material represents the dominant concern in distribution environments and in many manufacturing environments. Procurement activities can significantly impact the firm's bottom-line performance in terms of reduced material costs and inventories, improved quality and lead-time agility, and fewer disruptions stemming from stock-outs or delivery problems.

Purchase order processing represents a key business process within procurement and the organizing focus for further explanation. Related activities include the identification of vendor information, sourcing and agreement information, coordination efforts to meet game plan requirements, and receiving activities.

Vendor Information

Each vendor is defined in a vendor master file by a unique identifier. Buy-from and pay-to vendors require unique identifiers, and a vendor can optionally have one or more ship-from locations. Several data elements have particular significance to purchase order processing.

- *Shipping Information.* Shipping information pertaining to purchase orders includes the preferred shipping agent and service type.
- *Pay-to Vendor.* Each vendor can optionally have a designated pay-to vendor that acts as a default on purchase orders, where the pay-to vendor determines applicable pricing and discounts.
- *Attributes Related to G/L Account Number Assignment.* Account number assignment reflects the vendor posting group and business posting

group assigned a vendor. A vendor posting group defines accounts such as payables and service charges. A general business posting group works in combination with an item's product posting group to define accounts such as purchases and variances.

♦ *Vendor Hold Status.* A vendor hold status (termed a blocking status) can prevent recording of all transactions or selected transactions such as receipts and payments.

♦ *Biztalk Partner Information.* The ability to exchange documents electronically requires identification of the vendor as a Biztalk partner, the types of authorized documents, and rules for exchanging information. Outbound documents include purchase orders and request for purchase quote; inbound documents include a purchase order confirmation, purchase receipt, purchase quote, and a vendor's product catalog information.

Summarized information about a vendor can be viewed in several ways. A vendor's statistics include month-to-date (MTD) and year-to-date (YTD) values for purchases, invoices, and payments. The total value of purchases can be viewed across time, such as monthly or quarterly time increments. Entry statistics for a vendor include MTD and YTD transaction counts, such as the number of invoices, payments, and credit memos. Transaction detail can also be viewed by type of purchase document, such as outstanding quotes, purchase orders, and return orders.

Purchase Orders

Purchase orders for material items define scheduled receipts and provide one means to coordinate supply chain activities. Purchase order variations reflect outside operations and sales orders for drop-shipments and special orders. A line type defines other variations such as special charges.

The structure and life cycle of a purchase order serve as the starting points for further explanation. This section focuses on purchase orders for material items and highlights additional considerations such as order-related text and purchasing lead-time.

Purchase Order Structure and Life Cycle

The basic structure of a purchase order consists of header and line item information. As a reflection of this basic structure, the purchase order number and line number uniquely identify a scheduled receipt. The purchase order header identifies the buy-from vendor, which provides the basis for default values in other header fields such as pay-to vendor. The header information subsequently provides default values for line items, such as the planned delivery date. Summary information includes calculated order totals and a discount amount.

The life cycle of a purchase order consists of several steps, with two steps represented by an order status as explained below.

- *Open.* An open status indicates the purchase order is being created. The order header has been created, and one or more line items can be defined. Information can be changed on an open purchase order and a purchase order printed, but items cannot be received until the status is changed to released.

- *Released.* A released status indicates the purchase order information has been completely entered and authorizes receipt for all line items. Information cannot be changed on a released purchase order, but it can be manually reopened to allow changes. A released order allows receipt transactions and generation of receipt documents for warehouse management purposes.

A line item is automatically flagged as completely received when the received quantity equals the order quantity. This represents an implied closure, and receipts cannot exceed the order quantity. The order is automatically deleted when order quantities for all line items have been posted as completely received and invoiced. Historical information about a system-deleted purchase order can be viewed on the screens for posted receipts and posted invoices. A purchase order can be archived prior to deletion for data retention purposes, or for storing versions of a purchase order prior to changes.

There are several variations of a purchase order line, but each variation goes through the same life cycle statuses.

Purchase Order Variations for Material Items

Material items represent one type of purchase with an explicit designation of *item* as the purchase order line type. Material items can be designated for drop shipment and special order items that are linked to a sales order. Other variations include a kit of material items and an outside operation for a production order.

Special Order for Purchased Material   The purchase of a special order item stems from a sales order line item designated as a special order. Suggested requisitions for the same special order item can be combined or kept separate, based on a purchasing setup policy.

Drop Shipment for Purchased Material   The purchase of a drop-shipment item stems from a sales order line item designated as a drop ship-ment. The ship-to address information in the purchase order header comes from the sales order.

Kit of Material Items   A kit item is defined on the item master with an assembly list of components. A kit item can be priced, purchased, and received as a complete item. Alternatively, the purchase order line for a kit item can be exploded so that the kit's components are displayed as line items. This means the kit's components are priced, purchased, and received independently.

Outside Operation for a Production Order   The purchase order line item for an outside operation identifies the parent item and additional in-formation about the released production order. The additional information in-cludes the production order number and line number, and the operation number, operation description, and external work center defined in the or-der-dependent routing. The purchase order is created using the subcontracting worksheet. A receipt transaction transfers the purchase costs directly to the production order.

Other Types of Purchase Order Line Items

A purchase order for a material item represents one type of line item. Other line types can be designated, such as G/L charges, special charges, line item text, and fixed asset.

Line Item Text   Line item text can be manually entered as a description, or selected from a list of predefined standard text (identified by standard text codes). Multiple lines of line item text can be entered. The user can optionally override the description for the predefined standard text.

G/L Charges   A purchase order line for a G/L account typically repre-sents a non-inventoried expense item such as office supplies or professional services. It can also represent special charges that are not assigned to line items.

Item Charges   A purchase order line for an item charge code typically represents freight, landed costs, setup fees, a restocking charge, or other spe-cial charges. An item charge code must be predefined and associated with relevant G/L account numbers such as a purchase account. The amount of the item charges must be assigned to one or more purchase order line items in support of actual costing methods. Item charges can be manually or automatically assigned to other line items, with automatic assignment based on equal amounts per line or the proportionate value per line.

Fixed Asset   A fixed asset purchase can represent the acquisition or maintenance of a fixed asset, where the line item indicates the fixed asset identifier. Additional information must be indicated on the purchase order line item for an acquisition, and the receipt transaction updates information in the fixed assets application.

Purchase Order Considerations

The basic purchase order information defines a vendor, item, quantity, purchase price, planned receipt date, and ship-to location. Many situations require additional considerations, such as pricing and discounting, the use of textual explanations, vendor item numbers, and so forth.

Pricing and Discounting on a Purchase Order   The purchase price on a purchase order line represents the item's direct material cost per unit. A discount percentage or amount can be optionally specified for the line item, as well as a discount (or service charge) related to the total order. The item's purchase price and line discount can be manually entered, although the price initially defaults to the value of the item's last direct cost. The manual assignment typically applies to items purchased on a one-time or infrequent basis, such as special orders for non-stock items.

The automatic assignment of a purchase price and discount information reflects previously defined agreements with vendors. For example, purchase quotes or reverse auctions may be defined for a one-time purchase or a new item. Approved vendors and vendor agreement information are typically defined for more frequently purchased material, or a blanket purchase order can be used.

These approaches to sourcing and agreement information, and automatic pricing and discounting on purchase orders, are further explained in the next section.

Order-Related Text   Order-related text can be specified in three ways: as comments in the order header, as line item text, and as extended text carried forward from the item master.

◆ *Comments.* An order-related comment can be defined with multiple lines of free-form text. Each line can be assigned a user-defined code to sort and filter comments, such as filtering comments related to receiving or handling. Several policies determine whether comments will carry forward to related purchase documents. For example, the setup policies determine whether order-related comments are carried forward from a blanket order to purchase orders, and from a purchase order to invoices and receipts.

◆ *Line Item Text.* Line item text can be manually entered as a description, or selected from list of predefined standard text and optionally overridden.

◆ *Carry Forward of Item-Related Extended Text.* Extended text for an item can be selectively designated whether it will carry forward to purchase documents such as the purchase order and invoice. An item's extended text can be automatically added to purchase order line items (based on the item's policy) or a manual request to insert extended text on a line item can be made. The system considers the effectivity dates specified for the extended text. The extended text description can be overridden on the document.

Using Item Numbers vs. Cross-Reference Numbers A purchase order line item for material can identify the item number or a cross-reference number that represents the vendor item number or a catalog number.

Receipt Dates and Dock-to-Stock Handling Each purchase order line identifies a planned receipt date (when material should arrive on the receiving dock) and an expected receipt date (when material will be available in stock after safety lead-time and inbound warehouse handling time). These are sometimes referred to as the dock date and the stock date. Each line also has an order date when the order should be placed based on lead-time. Figure 6.1 illustrates these three dates and the time period segments.

The inbound warehouse handling time reflects the number of days to put away received material; it is defined by location. An item's safety lead-time represents an inspection lead-time or quarantine period expressed in days; it also represents a buffer against late deliveries from vendors. Planning calculations use the expected receipt date into stock as the basis for a scheduled receipt.

Each purchase order line also has a promised and requested receipt date that provides the basis for measuring on-time delivery by vendors. The dates specified in the order header (for promised, requested, and planned receipt dates) act as default values for each line item, and provide a means for mass updates of all line item receipt dates.

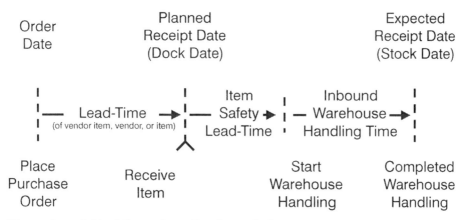

Figure 6.1   Critical Dates for a Purchase Order

Purchase Lead-Time   An item's purchase lead-time represents the notification period to place a purchase order and receive the item. It can be expressed in calendar days or working days (or weeks or months) and defined in three places—for the item, the vendor, or the vendor item—that provide increasing detail about lead-time. Planning calculations use the most detailed information available about an item's purchase lead-time.

Using a Template to Create Line Items   A short-cut approach for creating multiple line items involves a template, which is termed a *standard purchase code*. A template typically represents repeat orders although it may serve other creative purposes, such as viewing a group of related items that need to be purchased together. Various items can be grouped together; for example, to represent a matched set of components that stem from a vendor's production process, such as a molding or cutting operation. Various G/L account purchases can be grouped together as a template, such as a monthly breakdown of various contract cleaning and maintenance services.

Each template has a user-defined identifier, and defines a list of items and quantities. A template must be assigned to an individual vendor before usage. A template can be viewed and selected during purchase order entry, where selection automatically creates additional purchase order line items for the template's items and quantities. Templates can also be created on the fly during purchase order entry.

Reserving the Scheduled Receipt for a Sales Order   T h e scheduled receipt for a purchase order line item can be reserved for a sales order. This approach to a reservation avoids waiting until material has been received into inventory.

Creating a Purchase Order via Copying an Existing Purchase Document   The copy feature can be used to create purchase order line items or the entire order from an existing purchase document, such as another purchase order, quote, return order, or posted invoice. When copying only the line items, the system incrementally adds new line items with the same item, quantity, and ship-to location, and optionally recalculates prices and discounts based on the vendor and date. The incremental additions allow multiple copy efforts, and the system assigns a planned receipt date based on header information. Copying an entire document with its header information replaces the vendor and other header information, and also deletes existing lines.

Generating a Credit Memo or Return Order from a Purchase Order   Some situations require identification of items that must be returned or credited while a user is in the midst of purchase order entry. These items can be identified as purchase order line items with a negative quantity. The user can then choose whether to create a return order or a credit memo for the designated line items, and the designated lines are deleted from the purchase order.

Changing the Vendor on a Purchase Order   Changing the buy-from vendor for a purchase order (prior to ledger entries) has several impacts. The change results in new header information and an optional change for the pay-to vendor. Any existing line items are deleted and re-added with the applicable price and discount information, and the default ship-to location associated with the vendor.

Component Forecast Consumption by Purchase Orders   A purchase order line for a material item consumes the item's production forecast (if specified) to avoid doubled-up requirements. The line item's planned receipt date dictates forecast consumption logic within an implied forecast period. Note that a purchase order related to a blanket order consumes the blanket order quantity rather than a component forecast.

Sending a Purchase Order   A purchase order can be printed or faxed, printed to file and attached to an e-mail message, or sent via a Biztalk outbound document. An agreement concerning the Biztalk outbound document must be previously defined for the vendor; the system provides a warning when an agreement does not exist.

Handling Purchase Order Confirmations   An inbound Biztalk document for a purchase order confirmation can modify an existing purchase order, with a designated user notified via e-mail upon document receipt. The information includes the quantity, price, and receipt date for purchase order line items. Rules governing the inbound documents include manual versus automatic acceptance of the information. Another rule determines whether to automatically adjust information (such as quantity, price, and date) on the existing purchase order or to prompt for confirmation during manual acceptance.

Statistics for Purchase Orders   An order's statistics include calculated totals for costs, a calculated invoice discount that can be manually overridden, and calculated totals for quantity, volume, net weight, and gross weight. The statistics window also displays calculated tax amounts segmented by tax identifier.

Sourcing and Agreement Information

The extent of procurement activities to define source and agreement information for purchased material depends on the situation. For example, little effort may be expended on one-time orders for non-stock items, so that the purchase order itself defines an agreement. Some cases warrant solicitation and definition of one-time purchase quotes or reverse auctions from relevant vendors, where a quote or an auction winner defines the price basis for a purchase order. Considerable effort may be expended on vendor agreements for critical or frequently replenished material. The vendor agreement data provides the basis for automatically calculating prices and discounts on purchase orders, purchase quotes, blanket purchase orders, and other purchase documents. Some cases require the additional control provided by a blanket purchase order since it tracks an item's cumulative orders and receipts against the blanket and enforces maximum quantity limitations. This section summarizes these different approaches for the definition and use of sourcing and agreement information.

Preferred and Approved Vendors

Information about approved vendors and a preferred (or default) vendor can be defined for material items and on outside operations for manufactured items.

Preferred and Approved Vendor for a Purchased Material
The approved vendors for an item, or conversely the approved items for a vendor, represent cross-reference information. Information about an item's approved vendor includes the mapping between the internal and vendor item numbers and UM, and a vendor item description and purchase lead-time. An item's approved vendors can be viewed and selected on a suggested purchase.

An item's preferred vendor (also termed the primary or default vendor) represents location-specific information, and can be defined for each SKU. It serves as the default on suggested purchases for the location.

Preferred Vendor on an Outside Operation for a Manufactured Item   A subcontract manufactured item typically has a master routing with one or more subcontracted outside operations. A vendor performing outside operations is defined on the vendor master. An external work center is also defined that corresponds to the vendor, with the vendor number specified as the preferred vendor. The external work center can then be defined on a routing operation for the outside operation, with an operation-specific description (for subcontracted work to be performed) and per-unit price (that represents a form of a vendor agreement). Outside operations were explained in Chapter 3.

Vendor Agreements about Pricing and Discount

Various forms of vendor agreements can be expressed that affect pricing and discounts. An agreement may involve other aspects, such as freight charges, payment terms, or delivery dates. Further explanation focuses on pricing and discounts.

A vendor agreement's price information typically specifies consideration of factors such as date effectivities and quantity breakpoints, with information identified in a purchase price worksheet. Some agreements also specify discount percentages applicable to items, with information identified in a purchase line discount worksheet. And some agreements specify a discount percentage or service charge amount related to total order value, with information identified in a vendor-specific invoice discount worksheet. These three worksheets have parallel counterparts for sales purposes, as previously described in Chapter 2.

Purchase Price Worksheet   A purchase price worksheet defines agreed-upon item prices from a pay-to vendor, and provides automatic price assignment during purchase order entry. Item pricing often reflects one or more of the factors shown in Figure 6.2. For example, pricing by item and unit of measure can indicate different prices per item and per pallet, while pricing with date effectivities supports periodic updates for pricing agreements. Price assignment reflects the order date and a vendor policy defines whether prices include tax.

A simple price agreement requires one worksheet entry for each item. Additional worksheet entries would be required for variations in the purchased item's UM and quantity breakpoints. Note that a set of worksheet entries cannot be assigned a unique identifier such as an agreement number, but filters

Factor	Purchase Price Worksheet	Purchase Line Discount Worksheet
Pay to Vendor	X	X
Item and UM	X	X
Date Effectivity	X	X
Quantity Breakpoints	X	X
Currency Code	X	X
Related Policies	Vendor Policy: Prices Include Tax	

Figure 6.2   Purchase Prices and Line Discounts

can be used to view a subset of worksheet entries. The user can view available item prices during purchase order entry, such as viewing quantity breakpoints or future pricing to guide purchase decisions.

Purchase Line Discount Worksheet   A purchase line discount worksheet defines agreed-upon item discount percentages from a pay-to vendor, and provides automatic discount assignment during purchase order entry. An item's discount percentages often reflect one or more of the factors shown in Figure 6.2, such as discount percentages that vary by quantity breakpoint. The approach to defining worksheet entries mirrors the approach for a sales line discount worksheet, and the user can view available line discounts during purchase order entry to guide purchase decisions.

Discounts and Service Charges Related to Total Purchase Order Value   An invoice discount worksheet defines the agreed-upon invoice discount percentage and/or a service charge amount that applies to total order value for purchase orders placed with a vendor. Value breakpoints can also be defined. For example, an order exceeding $100 obtains a 10 percent discount while an order exceeding $500 obtains a 20 percent discount. A service charge example would be a $25 fee for an order less than $100. The service charge appears as a separate line on the purchase order (identified by the G/L account description for service charges). An invoice discount percentage and a service charge amount can both be defined for a vendor.

Purchase Quote

A purchase quote specifies the item price and quantity for one or more line items, and acts like a purchase order in many ways. For example, it uses the same approaches for pricing and discounting, cross reference identifiers, order-related text, purchase order variations, and templates. A purchase quote can also inherit vendor agreement information about pricing and discounts, and the quote's statistics window mirrors the summarized information for a purchase order. A request for quote can be sent via an outbound Biztalk document; a quote can also be created from an inbound Biztalk document.

A purchase quote can be converted or copied to a purchase order. When converting a quote, the system automatically assigns a separate purchase order number, creates the same line items as the quote, and deletes the quote. Copying the quote allows multiple usage.

Rules for Using Inbound Biztalk Documents

The ability to electronically exchange information requires identification of the vendor as a Biztalk partner, the authorized inbound and outbound documents, and the rules for exchanging information. A basic rule determines whether the vendor's transactions identify the internal item number, the vendor item number, or the common item number. Outbound documents include a purchase order and a request for purchase quote (generated from the Purchase Quote window). Inbound Biztalk documents include purchase quotes, purchase order confirmations, purchase receipts, and a vendor's product catalog. Several rules apply to each type of inbound Biztalk document, as illustrated below for a purchase quote.

An inbound Biztalk document for a purchase quote often represents the response to a request for quote. Rules governing the inbound purchase quote include manual versus automatic acceptance of the information, create new purchase quote versus modify existing purchase quote, and automatically adjust information (such as quantity and price) on an existing quote versus prompt for confirmation during manual acceptance.

Reverse Auctions and Handling a Request for Quote (RFQ)

A reverse auction represents an electronic approach to generating a request for quote (RFQ). It uses Internet commerce capabilities to send a request for quote to vendors, record their responses, and announce the winner and losers, and the winning response provides the basis for generating a purchase order. A reverse auction involves several steps: (1) define vendors as participants, (2) create a reverse auction, (3) choose vendor participants, (4) handle vendor responses, and (5) choose a winner and create a purchase order. Each reverse auction (identified by an auction number) identifies only one item and the Web site to which it belongs, and a status indicates whether it is unreleased, released, withdrawn, closed for offers, or completed with a purchase order generated.

Automatic creation of reverse auctions represents one approach for supporting order-point replenishment. Automatic creation of reverse auctions and identification of vendor participants (steps 2 and 3 above) can be performed for any item using a replenishment method based on order-point logic. A reverse auction is automatically created when any item's inventory falls below its reorder point. Automatic assignment of vendor participants reflects each item's preferred vendor, approved vendors, or all vendors flagged as agreeing to participate in reverse auctions.

Blanket Purchase Orders

A blanket purchase order specifies an item and aggregate quantity for one or more line items, where each item's aggregate quantity provides the basis for pricing and discounts. Each line item on a blanket order also specifies a shipment date that represents an approximation of when the aggregate quantity will be received. Many aspects are similar to a purchase order, such as the handling of order-related text and kit items.

Each purchase order line item related to a blanket order line item inherits its pricing and discount information and consumes the aggregate quantity. The cumulative purchase order quantities cannot exceed the aggregate quantity. The user can convert a blanket purchase order into a purchase order for the entire quantity or a partial quantity. This is sometimes referred to as a *release against the blanket purchase order*. The system automatically assigns a separate purchase order number, and identifies the originating blanket purchase order and line number on each purchase order line item. An alternative approach involves manual identification of the relevant blanket purchase order and line number when creating a purchase order line item. In either case, the system tracks the cumulative quantity shipped and invoiced for the blanket purchase order.

Coordinating Procurement Activities

A firm's game plans for saleable products and services provide the primary driver of procurement activities for material items. The game plans define item demands that form the first step in every purchase cycle. The nature of each game plan depends on the situation, as previously explained in Chapter 4, Sales and Operations Planning. For example, the game plan may involve sales forecast data, and planning calculations use a designated set of forecast data.

Planning calculations attempt to synchronize supplies with demands, and the underlying logic is reflected in several tools providing coordination of procurement activities. The primary coordination tool for a distribution environment consists of a requisition worksheet that suggests buyer actions to meet demand. In a manufacturing environment, the primary coordination tools consist of a planning worksheet and a subcontract worksheet that suggest buyer actions to meet demand.

Requisition Worksheet and Suggested Action Messages

A requisition worksheet identifies suggested action messages about new and existing purchase orders. The suggested actions can be analyzed, changed, and automatically implemented. The requisition worksheet also provides the starting point for execution of planning calculations. The requisition worksheet can have multiple versions identified by a user-defined template name. The use of different template names provides the ability to segment messages, as discussed below.

Execution of Planning Calculations   The user initiates execution of planning calculations for purchased items from the requisition worksheet. The planning calculations require a specified planning horizon and an order date. The order date typically reflects today's date and provides the basis for several calculations, such as identifying the order start date for new purchases triggered by order-point logic. Planning calculations are typically executed for all items, but they can be executed for a subset of items based on item number, location, or other filter.

In a manufacturing environment, planning calculations are typically executed from and displayed on a planning worksheet that also identifies suggested actions for new and existing production orders. From the planning worksheet, suggested action messages regarding purchased material can be copied to the requisition worksheet. Chapter 8 provides further explanation of the planning worksheet.

Suggested Action Messages   The requisition worksheet displays messages across the entire planning horizon specified for planning calculations. Planning calculations generate five types of messages regarding new and existing purchase orders as shown in Figure 6.3. Other message sources for a new purchase reflect sales order line items designated as a drop shipment or special order. The worksheet displays these messages based on two user-initi-

Message Source	Message	Implications Before Taking Action
Planning Calculations	New	Defaults to item's preferred vendor and vendor's agreement for price and discount; Making a release against a blanket order
	Cancel	Flexibility to cancel
	Reschedule	Flexibility to reschedule
	Change Quantity	Flexibility to change
	Reschedule & Change Quantity	Flexibility to change
Get Drop Shipment	New (for SO Drop Ship)	Defaults to item's preferred vendor and vendor's agreement for price and discount; Making a release against a blanket order; Confirm ship-to address info
Get Special Order	New (for SO Special Order)	Defaults to item's preferred vendor
Manually Entered	New (for Item or G/L Account)	

Figure 6.3   Suggested Action Messages on the Requisition Worksheet

ated processes to get the sales order information. A manually entered message for a new purchase represents a manual requisition for a G/L account or material item.

Segmenting Messages on the Requisition Worksheet   Action messages may be segmented into subsets to support more effective coordination efforts. Each subset is displayed on a different version (template name) of the requisition worksheet. Planning calculations must be initiated from the desired template name using a filter such as a location, so that the template name displays the location's suggested action messages. There are other examples of segmenting messages on template names. For example, a different template name can be used to segment action messages for special orders and drop shipments, or for situations requiring immediate action based on the get action message function.

Filtering and Analyzing Messages for New Purchases   Messages are typically filtered by buyer responsibility with additional filters to focus attention on the subset of critical actions. For example, a filter regarding buyer responsibility can be based on the Product Group Code or General Product Posting Group. Messages for new purchases are typically filtered and sorted based on order start date to focus attention on near-term purchases. Special attention is required for suggested purchases with an order start date or due date before today's date. Other approaches include filtering and sorting by vendor to improve the effectiveness of communications with the vendor.

The suggestion for a new purchase initially identifies the item's preferred vendor and a suggested price and discount based on agreements with the preferred vendor. The suggestion often requires further analysis.

- ◆ The item's approved vendors and their vendor agreement information may be viewed and selected.
- ◆ The vendor's blanket purchase order(s) for the item may be viewed, and a purchase order released against the blanket.
- ◆ The item's supply/demand information may be analyzed to understand the rationale behind the suggested purchase.

The information about each suggested purchase can be changed to reflect analysis efforts or communication with the vendor. A suggestion can also be flagged as confirmed; this provides reference-only information that steps have been undertaken.

Filtering and Analyzing Messages for Existing Orders   Messages are typically filtered by buyer responsibility with additional filters to focus attention on the subset of critical actions. Messages about existing orders are typically filtered and sorted based on order due date to focus attention on near-term activity. Special attention is required for existing orders with a due date before today's date. Other approaches include filtering and sorting by vendor to improve the effectiveness of communications with the vendor.

Suggestions about existing orders often require analysis of an item's supply/demand information to understand the rationale behind the suggestions and to assess the impact of not implementing a suggestion. The inability to reschedule an existing order, for example, may require changes to the sales order's shipment date. A suggestion can be flagged as having "no planning flexibility" to suppress further messages. As with a suggested purchase, suggestions about existing orders can be changed and/or flagged as confirmed.

Implementing Suggested Action Messages   Messages are automatically implemented based on the *accept action message* flag and the user-initiated process to carry out action messages. Suggested messages further out in the planning horizon should be deleted or not accepted to avoid inadvertent implementation.

Planning Worksheet and Suggested Action Messages

In a manufacturing environment, planning calculations are typically executed from and displayed on a planning worksheet. The planning worksheet displays suggested actions related to purchase, transfer, and production orders. Suggestions regarding purchased items can be generated, analyzed, and implemented on the planning worksheet using the same approaches described above for the requisition worksheet. In particular, implementing suggestions can be carried out for just purchase orders or just production orders. This approach represents a combined buyer/planner role.

Alternatively, suggestions about purchased material can be copied to a specified requisition worksheet template name. This approach represents separate roles for the buyer and planner. In either case, the suggestions regarding manufactured items impact procurement activity. Chapter 8 provides further explanation of the planning worksheet.

Subcontracting Worksheet and Suggested Action Messages

Some manufacturing environments involve purchasing of outside operations. The subcontracting worksheet displays suggestions for new purchases of outside operations for released production orders, and is also used to create these purchase orders. A user-initiated process calculates new subcontract suggestions based on outside operations in the order-dependent routings, but does not generate other types of suggestions such as reschedule messages.

Each suggestion identifies information about the operation description, the related production order and external work center, and the preferred vendor for the external work center. Information can be changed such as overriding the vendor and unit cost. Each message can be automatically implemented based on the *accept action message* flag and the user-initiated process to carry out action messages.

Methods for Creating a Purchase Order

In addition to manual entry, a purchase order for a material item can be created from a requisition worksheet, a planning worksheet, a purchase quote, a blanket purchase order, a reverse auction, a purchase return or credit memo. A purchase order for an outside operation can be created from the subcontracting worksheet.

Receiving Activities and Returns to Vendor

Receipts represent the completion of purchase order processing, and also the starting point for returns to vendor.

Purchase Receipts   Different approaches can be taken to report receiving activity for material items. The basic approach focuses on reporting receipts against line items on an individual purchase order. The received quantities and their stocking locations are entered on the purchase order window (or an equivalent version for receiving purposes). The window displays default values for each line item's quantity and stocking location to help minimize data entry efforts. Posting the data updates inventory balances. Sometimes the vendor's invoice accompanies the material, so that posting can optionally create the purchase invoice. Chapter 7 describes other approaches for reporting receipts.

Purchase Returns   Material received against a purchase order sometimes must be returned to the vendor. Returns cannot be recorded on the purchase order window. However, a purchase order line item entered with a negative quantity can be converted to a return order or credit memo.

A purchase return order provides a structured approach for handling returns to vendor and creation of the associated credit memo. Its structure and life cycle mirror that of a purchase order. The order header identifies the vendor, return address, and vendor's return authorization code. Each line item identifies the item and quantity to be returned, and related information such as reason code, price, and return date. Reservations can be made for the specific inventory to be returned.

When material must be returned to a vendor, there is frequently a requirement to purchase replacement material. A return order (or credit memo) line item with a negative quantity can be converted to a purchase order to obtain the replacement material.

The sales return window includes the ability to create a purchase return order for returning customers' goods to the responsible vendor. It can also create a new purchase order for getting replacement items from the vendor.

Case Studies

Case #31: Multistep Receiving and Vendor Performance
The All-and-Anything company required a multistep receiving procedure that required extensions to standardized functionality. The procedure involves handling inbound material before and after recognition of a purchase order re-

ceipt. First, a purchased item could be assigned a receipt routing that defined the receiving steps, where one of the routing operations can be designated as the basis for recording the inventory receipt. Second, an item's yield percentage and inspection lead-time could be specified, and scheduled receipts were factored by planning calculations. Third, the item's yield factor and receipt routing were optionally included in cost calculations. Fourth, an inventory status (of on-hand, on-hold, and in-inspection) was added to inventory records and recognized by planning calculations. Fifth, unit completions by operation served to update purchase order receipts, with special handling for a scrap quantity (such as creating a return to vendor). The reporting of good and scrap quantities also provided the basis for vendor performance ratings concerning quality.[1]

Case #32: Buyer Action Messages   The All-and-Anything company wanted to improve coordination of purchasing activities by enhancing suggested action messages. Building on the concept of buyer responsibility assigned to items and purchase order line items, they extended the scope of suggested action messages on the requisition worksheet (and planning worksheet). Additional message types included follow-up on past-due receipt, suggested releases against a blanket order, and reviewing quotes and blanket orders about to expire. Message filters were also defined for various message types.[2]

Case #33: Conditional Release of Lot-Traced Material in Process Manufacturing   The Batch Process company purchased lot-traced material that required time-consuming compliance tests and could go into production subject to conditional release but not be shipped. As part of their customizations, they defined a lot attribute to identity status (such as a conditional release) that allowed usage, and prevented shipment of a lot-traced product comprised of lot-traced components with a conditional release.

Case #34: Vendor Schedules   The Equipment company wanted to improve coordination with key suppliers by providing visibility of anticipated purchases, which the supplier could then use as forecasted demand. A customized vendor schedule report identified existing purchase orders and suggested

---

[1] See *Maximizing Your ERP System* for further explanation of vendor performance ratings (pp. 263–265), inventory status (p. 271), receiving inspection (pp. 319–320), item yield (pp. 124 and 320), and coordination of receiving inspection activities (pp. 324–325).

[2] See *Maximizing Your ERP System* for further explanation of buyer responsibility (pp. 116–117), types of buyer action messages (pp. 261–262), and message filters (pp. 268–269).

purchases for items supplied by the vendor. Each item's quantities were displayed in weekly buckets for an eight-week horizon and monthly buckets thereafter, with identification of suggested orders based on the item's preferred vendor. A report refinement supported a multisourced item, where an additional field for the item's approved vendors identified a supplied percentage that factored suggested purchase quantities.

Case #35: Multiple Subcontractors The Fabricated Products company required several outside operations to produce an item. Several different contractors could perform each outside operation. Different levels in the bill of material defined each stage of manufacturing—one stage for each outside operation—and a production order was created for each stage. Each subcontractor was defined as a separate location, so that supplied material and a completed item could be identified by inventory location. Material was shipped to the subcontractor performing the first operation and auto-deducted based on production order output. The output was placed into the location corresponding to the next subcontractor. This approach allowed planning calculations to synchronize supplied material with the subcontractor performing each outside operation, and also minimized transaction processing about material movements between subcontractors.

Executive Summary

Purchased material represents the dominant concern in distribution environments and in many manufacturing environments. The supply chain activities for purchased material reflect demands stemming from the S&OP game plans for saleable products. In addition to purchase orders for stocked material, purchase order variations include drop shipments, special orders, kit items, and outside operations. Sourcing and agreement information can be defined, including preferred and approved vendors, vendor agreements about prices and discounts, purchase quotes, reverse auctions, and blanket purchase orders. Planning calculations help coordinate procurement activities by communicating suggested action messages on a requisition worksheet. These messages suggest new purchases and changes to existing purchase orders, such as rescheduling or canceling an order. The case studies highlight variations in purchase order processing, including multistep receiving procedures and the use of vendor schedules.

Chapter 7

Warehouse Management

Warehouse management involves the physical storage and movement of products in the supply chain. This includes inventory management within a location, the handling of outbound and inbound shipments, quality management considerations such as incoming inspection, issuing components to production orders and handling output in a manufacturing environment, and handling transfer orders between locations in a multisite environment. Various terms (such as inventory management or distribution management) are used to refer to these activities, and responsibility for these activities may be assigned to one or several functional areas. For simplicity's sake, further explanations use the terms warehouse management function and warehouse personnel, and several synonyms for a location—such as warehouse, plant, and site—will be used interchangeably.

The requirements for coordinating and reporting warehouse management activities vary from company to company, and between sites within a company. For example, a smaller firm often has simpler requirements and warehouse personnel can handle put-away requirements in their head. Other firms have larger warehouse facilities with more complex requirements for putting away and picking material, and warehouse personnel need explicit instructions on what to do. This argues for a contingency approach for modeling and managing warehouse management activities. This chapter explains three levels of functionality for managing warehouse activities: basic, intermediate, and advanced.

The starting point for explaining the basic level of warehouse management functionality involves the definition of inventory locations and the approach to inventory transactions. Explanations for each additional level of functionality involve revisiting the warehouse management policies for a location and the impact on inventory transactions.

Basic Functionality for Warehouse Management

Warehouse management functionality requires definition of locations and bins. It also involves several types of inventory transactions. These include inventory adjustments, movements, and physical inventory counts, and transactions related to sales order shipments, purchase order receipts, and production order issues and output.

Defining a Location and Bins

An inventory stocking location is uniquely identified by a location and bin, where a location can have one or more bins. The basic information about a location includes address and communication data and several warehouse management policies. The policies include the shop calendar of working days, the average number of days for handling inbound and outbound shipments, and the use of bins. Bin codes can be used to suggest a walk-through sequence for picking and put-away purposes, so that bin code assignment requires careful consideration. Bins can be defined one-at-a-time or via a mass creation approach. The mass creation approach uses a bin naming system (such as segmentation by rack, section, and level) and number ranges (such as the number range for racks) to automatically create bin codes on a bin creation worksheet.

A bin can be designated as blocked. The blocked status is intended to prevent all inventory transactions, just inbound transactions, or just outbound transactions. The need for preventing inventory transactions, for example, may represent quarantined material for quality management purposes. The inventory in a blocked bin is still considered available by planning calculations.

Authorized Locations for an Item and Stockkeeping Units (SKUs)
A relationship between locations and an item can be defined. An item can have one or more authorized locations (termed *stockkeeping units*) for the purpose of defining location-specific planning, costing, and warehouse stocking data. Chapters 2 and 3 described this location-specific information about items.

Authorized Bins and the Default Bin for an SKU
A relationship between bins and an SKU can be defined. An SKU can have one or more authorized bins (termed *fixed bins*) for stocking purposes; all other bins are viewed as unauthorized (and are termed *floating bins*) for the item. One fixed bin can also be designated as the preferred bin (termed the *default bin*). However, a warehouse management policy determines whether the default bin is manually assigned or automatically updated based on the last put-away transaction. An SKU's default bin can be manually overridden. The system displays the

default bin for every inventory transaction (thereby minimizing additional data entry) and it provides the basis for sorting information in bin location sequence (thereby improving efficiencies for pick and put-away purposes).

Types of Inventory Transactions

Warehouse management involves complete and accurate reporting of inventory transactions. The basic inventory transactions include inventory adjustments, movements, receipts, shipments, production order issues and output, and physical inventory counts. The basic inventory transactions are summarized in Figure 7.1. Chapter 9 covers inventory transactions related to transfer orders.

Inventory Adjustments   Inventory adjustments serve a variety of purposes, such as loading initial inventory balances, reporting inventory corrections, and reporting scrap. Inventory adjustments are recorded on the Item Journal window. An adjustment type can be positive or negative, and each adjustment minimally identifies an item, quantity and UM, stocking location (location and bin), and a user-assigned document number for reference purposes. An item's tracking policy enforces identification of the lot and/or serial numbers. For a negative adjustment, the user can view an item's existing inventory

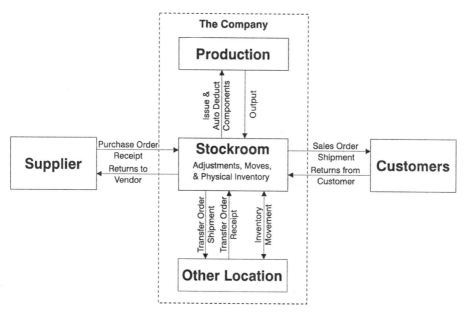

Figure 7.1   Basic Inventory Transactions

by bin and by lot/serial number. The adjustment entries in an Item Journal can be maintained and printed prior to posting.

Inventory Movements   Inventory movements between bins within a location and movements between locations are recorded on the Item Reclassification Journal window. Each movement minimally identifies an item, quantity and UM, the old and new stocking locations (site and bin), and a document number for reference purposes. An item's tracking policy enforces identification of the lot and/or serial numbers. The movement entries in an Item Reclassification Journal can be maintained and printed prior to posting.

Inventory movement transactions are required for a variety of purposes. For example, they can record movements to restock primary bins from overflow or bulk storage bins. Other examples involve moving material from the receiving dock to a bin in the stockroom, or from a stockroom bin to a staging area prior to sales order shipment. The use of warehouse documents provides an alternative approach to recording these inventory movements. For example, a put-away document records material movement from a receiving dock to a bin in the stockroom.

Physical Inventory and Cycle Counting   Physical inventories help ensure valid financial reporting of inventory value. Cycle counting can accomplish the same objective and help identify the source of inventory errors.

The preparation and reporting for a physical inventory are performed on the Physical Inventory Journal window. The first step involves defining a batch name for the physical inventory and the identification of items to be counted. Items can be manually added to the batch or automatically added via a calculate inventory function. In most cases, all items and their stocking locations with an inventory balance should be added automatically. Printing a list of these items to be counted (such as the Physical Inventory List report) or a card for each item provides a turnaround document for reporting actual counts. In either case, the turnaround document should provide information about the item, each stocking location with an inventory balance, and (if applicable) the lot and serial numbers. Actual counts that identify differences can then be entered for the batch name on the Physical Inventory Journal window. The information can be reviewed via test reports and then posted.

The preparation and reporting for a cycle count follows a similar pattern, but requires several initial preparation steps. The initial preparation involves two steps for assigning a cycle count frequency and a next counting period to each item. A user-defined code defines the desired counting frequency per year (such as 4) and this code must be assigned to each item. Using a function to calculate counting period, the system calculates the date range constituting the item's next counting period.

Preparation and reporting for a cycle count are performed on the Physical Inventory Journal window as well. The first step involves defining a batch name for the cycle count and the identification of items to be counted. Items can be manually added to the batch or selected from a list of items that need to be counted (based on today's date and the date range of the items' next accounting period). The list of items displays the date last counted and the list gets calculated via a calculate counting period function. After selecting or manually adding items to the batch, the batch can be printed as a turnaround document for reporting actual counts. Actual counts that identify differences can then be entered for the batch name on the Physical Inventory Journal window. The information can be reviewed via test reports and then posted. An extra step must be performed after posting cycle counts: an item's next counting period must be recalculated on the item master using the same function mentioned above to calculate counting period.

Purchase Order Receipts   The receiving process may involve a single transaction for recording receipts or two transactions—one transaction to receive the material and a second transaction to move the material to its stocking location. These are called a one-step and two-step receiving process, respectively.

The basic approach focuses on reporting receipts against line items on an individual purchase order, and the receipt transaction typically represents a one-step receiving process. In many cases, the printed purchase order provides a turnaround document for reporting each item's actual receipt quantity and placement in a bin location. The receipt information is entered on the Purchase Order window (or an equivalent Order Receipt window) and posting the data creates a posted receipt and updates inventory balances. For correcting mistakes, the user can undo a purchase order receipt (using the Posted Receipts window) anytime prior to posting the vendor's invoice. When a vendor's invoice accompanies the material, it can also be entered at the same time as the receipt transaction.

Sales Order Shipments   The shipping process may involve a single transaction for recording shipment or two transactions—one transaction to pick and move material from a stockroom, and a second transaction to record shipment. These are called a one-step and two-step shipping process, respectively.

Picking and shipping activities focus on individual sales orders and the shipment transaction typically represents a one-step shipping process. In many cases, the printed sales order serves as a pick list and turnaround document for recording actual quantities shipped from stocking locations. Actual shipment data is entered on the Sales Order window (or an equivalent version for shipping purposes), and posting the data creates a posted shipment and updates inventory balances. For correcting mistakes, the user can undo a sales order shipment (using the Posted Shipments window) anytime prior to posting the sales invoice. Some situations require an invoice to accompany the shipment, so that posting can optionally create the sales invoice.

Production Order Issues and Output   The component requirements for a released production order include manually picked and auto-deducted components. A printed pick list provides one method for communicating the need to manually pick components for a production order. The pick list identifies components in the order-dependent bill. Actual component usage can then be entered and posted on the Consumption Journal window. This window is also used to report over- and underconsumption of auto-deducted components.

Components are typically issued from the manufacturing location specified for the production order line item. However, the source location for a component can be manually specified in the order-dependent bill. In some cases, the source location for components is always different than the manufacturing location for the production order. This alternate source of components can be designated for the SKU (using the policy on components at location) so that the order-dependent bill and planning calculations correctly identify component requirements.

Reporting actual output from a production order includes the quantity completed (both good and scrapped) and the placement of good items in a stocking location. Actual quantities and stocking locations are entered and posted on the Output Journal window.

Other Transactions   Other transactions shown in Figure 7.1 include returns to vendor, returns from customers, and transfer order shipments to and receipts from another location. Production order issues and output represent inventory transactions related to an outside operation.

Transaction Audit Trails   The system automatically maintains several audit trails related to inventory transactions, as described below.

♦ *Inventory Transaction Audit Trail for an Item.* An item's transaction audit trail identifies every inventory-related transaction, including transactions related to adjustments, sales orders, purchase orders, component issues to a production order, and output from a production order. Additional transactions reflect physical inventory. These aspects of an inventory transaction audit trail are termed *item ledger entries* and *physical inventory entries,* respectively, and the transaction type is termed *ledger entry type.*

An item's inventory transaction audit trail may include lot and/or serial numbers based on the item tracking policies. The system provides separate access to these item tracking entries.

• *Financial Transaction Audit Trail for an Item.* The financial equivalents for an inventory transaction audit trail are termed *item value entries.* An item's value entries identify and segment the financial impact for each inventory-related transaction, such as segmenting a purchase order receipt into direct and indirect costs. With standard costing, item-related value entries also identify variances and changes to standard cost that revalue existing inventory.

Current inventory balances can be viewed in several ways, such as by item, SKU, bin, and item tracking summary.

Intermediate Functionality for Warehouse Management

Several inventory transactions involve orders, and an order-based approach to reporting warehouse activities was described above. An alternative approach involves the use of documents (rather than orders) to coordinate and report warehouse activities. The document-based approach is oriented toward warehouse activities, such as receipts, put-aways, picks, and shipments. For example, receipts can be reported against a receipt document that represents an incoming shipment containing material from many purchase orders. The document-based approach provides several advantages over the order-based approach, such as supporting receipt and shipment transactions for multiple orders, a two-step receipt process, and a two-step shipping process. It supports receiving inspection procedures that constrain usage until material has been put away. It identifies shortages related to incoming material and notifies availability for outgoing requirements.

The document-based approach represents an intermediate level of functionality for supporting warehouse management activities. Several warehouse management policies determine whether a location will use a document- or an order-based approach for handling receipts, put-aways, picks, and shipments.

Warehouse Management Policies for Using Documents

Several warehouse management policies determine whether documents or orders provide the basis for reporting inventory transactions at a given location. A separate policy can be specified for handling receipts, put-aways, picks, and/or shipments. The possible combinations of policies can become confusing, especially when the combinations lead to different terms for documents.

For simplicity's sake, further explanation only covers scenarios involving all four documents.

One of the item tracking policies for lot- or serial-traced items affects the use of documents for reporting inventory transactions. The policy determines whether warehouse documents (such as a receipt document) must identify the lot and serial numbers.

Purchase Order Receipts and Put-Aways

Purchase order receiving activities can be handled as a two-step process using both a receipt document and a put-away document, or as a one-step process using just one of these documents. Further explanation focuses on the two-step process. In its simplest form, the two-step receiving process involves creating and posting a receipt document to receive items into one bin, and then registering the associated put-away document to move items (via take-and-place instructions) into their stocking location. This simple approach only requires a few keystrokes to update information when the default values (such as an SKU's default bin) do not require corrections.

Receipt Document   A receipt document is designed to support receiving activities, since it displays purchase order line items with sorting to improve receiving efficiencies (such as sorting by item or purchase order) . Each receipt document has a unique identifier and can be viewed and maintained on the Warehouse Receipt window. There are two basic variations for creating and using a receipt document.

- *Generate from the Purchase Order Window.* The buyer generates the receipt document for each released purchase order, thereby communicating anticipated receipts to warehouse personnel. The list of receipt documents provides workload visibility for the warehouse.

- *Generate from the Warehouse Receipt Window.* The warehouse personnel create a receipt document for an incoming shipment. The creation process provides an opportunity to view anticipated receipts. After creating a new receipt document, the user can view all anticipated receipts or a subset based on filters such as vendor and planned receipt date. The visibility represents a schedule of anticipated receipts. The user can then select purchase orders or use filters to select specific line items to be included on the receipt document.

  This approach is typically used to identify all items within an incoming shipment for the location. The items may represent line items from multiple purchase orders. Some people term this a *consolidated receipt document.*

In either case, the receipt document provides a means for reporting actual receipt quantity and placement in a receiving bin location. The receiving bin location typically represents the receiving dock or a receiving inspection area. The line items on a receipt document can be sorted, such as sequencing by item or purchase order. The printed version provides a turnaround document for recording item tracking data (if applicable) and differences in actual receipt quantities, and the information can be entered on the Warehouse Receipt window. Posting the receipt document updates inventory balances and the quantity received for each related purchase order. It also automatically generates an associated put-away document.

Put-Away Document A put-away document is designed to support put-away activities, since it displays each item's default stocking location and can be sorted to improve put-away efficiencies (such as sequencing by bin location). In a two-step process, it is automatically created after posting the associated receipt document and contains the same line items. It has a unique identifier and can be viewed and maintained on the Warehouse Put-Away window. Each line item includes "take-and-place instructions" to take the item from the receiving bin location and place it in a stocking location (such as the item's default bin). The printed version provides a turnaround document for recording differences in actual placement, and information can be entered on the Warehouse Put-Away window. Placing an item in two stocking locations requires an additional line on the put-away document to identity the separate quantity and bin location. This is termed splitting a line. Registering the put-away document moves the inventory for all line items.

The advanced warehouse management functionality provides a rules-based approach for suggested placement of items into a bin location, rather than just using the default bin as a put-away suggestion.

Sales Order Picking and Shipment

Sales order shipping activities can be handled as a two-step process using both a pick document and a shipment document, or as a one-step process using just one of these documents. Further explanation focuses on the two-step process. In its simplest form, the two-step shipping process involves creating a ship document and its associated pick document, registering the pick document that provides "take-and-place instructions" for moving items from their stocking location to a staging bin, and then posting the shipment document when items are shipped. This simple approach only requires a few keystrokes when the default values (such as an SKU's default bin) do not require correction.

Further explanation starts with creation of the shipment document and its associated pick document, then returns to the use of the shipment document for reporting shipments.

Shipment Document as a Starting Point   A shipment document provides the starting point for coordinating picking and shipping activities. It has a unique identifier and can be viewed and maintained on the Warehouse Shipment window. There are two basic variations for creating and using a shipment document.

- ◆ *Generate from the Sales Order Window.* The order entry function generates a shipment document for each sales order to communicate anticipated shipments to warehouse personnel. The list of shipment documents provides workload visibility for the warehouse.

- ◆ *Generate from the Warehouse Shipment Window.* The warehouse personnel create a shipment document for an outbound shipment. The creation process for a shipment document provides an opportunity to view anticipated shipments. After creating a new shipment document, the user can view all anticipated shipments or a subset based on filters such as shipping agent and planned shipment date. The visibility represents a schedule of anticipated shipments. The user can then select sales orders or use filters to select specific line items to be included on the shipment document.

    This approach is typically used to identify all items for an outbound shipment, such as an outgoing truckload for a specific shipping agent. The items can represent line items from multiple sales orders.

In either case, the shipment document provides the basis for creating an associated pick document and tracking the status of related activities. This pick document coordinates the gathering of material in preparation for shipment, so that shipments can be reported using the shipment document.

Pick Document   The pick document is designed to support picking activities with sorting to improve warehouse personnel efficiencies (such as sequencing by bin location for sweep picking purposes). It has a unique identifier and can be viewed and maintained on the Warehouse Pick window. In a two-step shipping process, it is created from an associated shipment document and contains the same line items. Each line includes "take-and-place instructions" to take inventory from the item's stocking location and place it in a staging bin location. The printed version provides a turnaround document for recording item tracking numbers (if applicable) and differences in actual quantities and bin locations, and information can be entered on the Warehouse Pick window. Taking an item from two stocking locations, or taking different units of measure, requires an additional line in the pick document to identify the separate quantity, UM, and bin location. Registering the pick document moves the inventory for all line items. It also automatically updates the associated shipment document with the quantities to ship.

Shipment Document as the Shipping Transaction   A shipment document is designed to support shipping activities, since it can be sorted to improve warehouse personnel efficiencies (such as sequencing by sales order or ship-to address). In a two-step shipping process, it is automatically updated with the quantities to ship based on registering the associated pick document. The printed version provides a turnaround document for recording differences in actual shipment, and information can be entered on the Warehouse Shipment window. This includes information about the shipping agent and service that will transport all line items, and an optional external document number such as the tracking number assigned by the shipping agent.

The shipment document provides the basis for tracking the status of related activities. The status indicates whether material has been partially or completely picked, and partially or completely shipped.

Posting the shipment document updates inventory balances and the quantity shipped for each related sales order. Posting can also generate the associated invoices for each related sales order. The system deletes a shipment document after all line items have been completely shipped and invoiced.

Other Transactions

The two-step receipt process (using the receipt and put-away documents) applies to sales returns and transfer order receipts. The two-step ship process (using the shipment and pick documents) applies to purchase returns and transfer order shipments. The pick document applies to the components for a released production order and is generated from the order. After reporting the output of a production order, an internal put-away and an associated put-away document can be created for moving inventory.

Assigning Responsibility for a Document

Responsibility for each document can be identified by an individual warehouse employee (termed the *assigned user ID*). The employee can then filter documents to focus on responsibilities and anticipated workload.

Alternatively, the employee can select any unassigned document and take responsibility for it.

Advanced Functionality for Warehouse Management

One of the distinguishing characteristics of more complex warehouse environments involves put-away rules. Other distinguishing characteristics include optimal sequencing of pick activities, bin replenishment based on min-max logic, and special equipment requirements for put-aways and picks. This section highlights some of the advanced functionality that addresses the requirements of more complex warehouse environments. A warehouse management policy—termed *directed put-away and pick*—determines whether a location can employ the advanced functionality.

A Rules-Based Approach to Directed Put-Aways

Many warehouse environments use an informal approach to put-away rules. An informal approach takes different forms, such as a bulletin board notice or a procedures manual, but it is not embedded in system logic. This means warehouse personnel must work out the rules in their head. Several examples of put-away rules will be used to illustrate how to embed put-away rules in the system logic.

Basic Put-Away Rules   The basic put-away rules for received material involve a form of cascade logic, as illustrated by the following rules used by one warehouse manager.

◆ *Rule #1.* Put the item in bins that need to be replenished. The bin's inventory has fallen below the SKU's minimum quantity, and the suggested put-away quantity reflects min-max bin replenishment logic.

◆ *Rule #2.* Put the item in an authorized bin. First try to put it in an empty bin. If that doesn't work, put it in a bin with existing inventory of the item. Try to match the unit of measure (e.g., put pallets with pallets, pieces with pieces), otherwise mix the units of measure.

◆ *Rule #3.* Put the item in an unauthorized bin. First try to put it in a bin with existing inventory of the item, preferably matching the unit of measure but mixing units if necessary. Otherwise, just put the item anywhere that you see fit.

These basic rules are termed a put-away template. One or more put-away templates can be defined to represent variations of the basic rules, and then assigned to individual SKUs or to the location (which then acts as a default when an SKU does not have an assigned template).

Other Put-Away Rules The warehouse manager in this example had several other put-away rules, as illustrated below, that are expressed as take-and-place instructions on the put-away documents.

- *Rule #4.* Check the shortage list. If shortages exist for a received item, put it in the "hot items" bin so it will be immediately available for shipping to a sales order or picking for a production order.
- *Rule #5.* Check bin ranking. Put the item in the highest ranked bin; then put it in lower ranked bins.
- *Rule #6.* Enforce requirements for environmental conditions. Put items in cold storage if they need it.
- *Rule #7.* Enforce weight and cubage limitations for a bin. Account for the bin limitations and the SKU's weight and cubage when you put items away.
- *Rule #8.* Unpack (or repack) the received material so it matches the desired put-away unit of measure. For example, unpack a pallet and stock it in pieces.

Other Considerations

Other considerations for the advanced functionality include improvements in the picking process and the impact on inventory transactions.

Improving the Picking Process The picking process sometimes requires unpacking (or repacking) stocked material into a different unit of measure to match the customer's desired UM. This is communicated via take-and-place instructions on a pick document. Bin ranking can also help sequence the picking process.

Impact on Inventory Transactions Several tools are only supported by the advanced functionality. These include three different worksheets—for picking, put-away, and movement—to group together related orders into a document. The advanced functionality also requires the use of different windows for reporting inventory adjustments, movements, and physical inventory counts. These warehouse transactions act the same as previously described inventory transactions, but an additional step must be taken to update inventory balances.

Case Studies

Case #36: Stockroom Action Messages
The All-and-Anything company wanted to improve coordination of stockroom activities by providing suggested action messages in one place. The customized window built on the existing functionality concerning receipt, pick, put-away, and ship documents that communicated needed stockroom action. It also identified new types of messages, such as the need to review past-due picks and shipments, review receipts for items with shortages, replenish inventory in bins based on min-max quantities, review auto-deduction errors, review lot expiration for stocked material, and perform cycle counts.

Case #37: Quality Management
The quality manager at the Batch Process company wanted to extend the concept of inventory status associated with blocking transactions for a bin's inventory. The basic types of inventory status included on-hand, in-inspection, and on-hold, although other user-defined inventory statuses could be added. The impact of each inventory status could be designated in terms of planning calculations and usability. For example, planning calculations ignored on-hold inventory while issue transactions were prevented for in-inspection inventory. Quality management required limited access for inventory transactions related to dispositions of in-inspection inventory. Quality management also required identification of the source of material placed into in-inspection status, such as the purchase order for received material, to provide quality metrics.[1]

Quality management required a historical genealogy of lot- and serial-traced items. The window displayed downward traceability information for a specified item and lot (or serial) number, using an indented bill format to indicate each link in the tracking chain. The window could also display upward traceability information, using an indented where-used format to view tracking history for a specified item and lot (or serial) number. These formats enabled the quality manager to view a complete history from end-item shipment to a component's purchase order receipt, with drill-down to the details for a specific lot (or serial) number.

Case #38: ASNs and Bar Code Labels
A key customer of the Consumer Products company required an Advanced Ship Notice (ASN) and bar-coded shipping labels for each shipment. The shipping labels identified the cartons and pallets within a shipment. The ASN information included basic

---

[1] See *Maximizing Your ERP System* for further explanation of inventory status and quality management (pp. 271–272, 276–277, and 296–297).

data about the shipment number and customer PO number(s) included in the shipment, as well as content data about the items (for a standard pack approach) or about the pallets, cartons, and items within cartons (for a pick-and-pack approach). These represent the basic variations in the hierarchical data structure for the ANSI X-12 856 transaction for ASNs. The combination of ASN and bar-coded labels enable the customer to quickly and accurately process material receipts via bar-code scanning, and to anticipate incoming material for put-away purposes.

Case #39: Data Collection System The Distribution company implemented an automated data collection system along with the advanced functionality of directed put-away and picking. Using the automatic data capture system (ADCS) capabilities, warehouse personnel using hand-held devices recorded all inventory transactions. Each transaction required definition of the user interface for the device, including a miniform, handheld functions, and data exchanges. A miniform defined the amount of information displayed on the hand-held device, such as a list of documents the user can select from and the errors (or affirmations) about activities being recorded by the user.

Case #40: Shortage Reports The warehouse manager at the Equipment company wanted a shortage report that simplified and extended the functionality associated with cross-docking opportunities. This report required a clear definition of shortages related to sales orders, production orders, and other orders. It also involved on-line notification of shortages when warehouse personnel processed receipts or handled put-away of material that cleared inspection, so they could issue the material to cover the shortage. The format for notifications (and shortage reports) included shortages by item and shortages by order.

Case #41: Warehouse Management Reports The warehouse manager at the Fabricated Products company wanted to use daily usage rates to extend the usefulness of existing reports. These new reports used historical and projected daily usage rates to calculate the ABC classifications for items, identify excess inventory, and calculate min-max quantities for bin replenishment and planning data purposes. Additional reports were also developed to provide inventory accuracy metrics (based on cycle count feedback) and shortage lists.

Executive Summary

Warehouse management involves the physical storage and movement of products in the supply chain. This includes inventory management within a location, the handling of inbound and outbound shipments, issuing components and handling output related to production orders, and quality management considerations such as incoming inspection. The requirements for coordinating and reporting warehouse management activities vary between companies and locations. Therefore, different levels of functionality—basic, intermediate, and advanced—are required for supporting these activities. The basic inventory transactions, for example, include inventory adjustments, movements, cycle counting, purchase order receipts, sales order shipments, and production order issues and output. A shift toward the use of warehouse documents—for receipts, put-aways, picks, and shipments—provides several advantages and represents an intermediate level of functionality. The advanced functionality includes a rules-based approach to directed put-aways, such as enforcing environmental storage conditions or accounting for bin limitations about weight and volume. The case studies highlight extensions to warehouse management, such as reports for quality management and warehouse management purposes.

Chapter 8

Production Order Processing

Production represents the heart of most manufacturers and their distinctive competency. A separate functional area termed production activity control is typically responsible for coordinating the execution of production activities. These activities are driven by the firm's S&OP (sales and operations planning) game plans.

Manufacturing environments can have a wide range of production activities. Many of these variations in production activities can be modeled using bill of material and routing information, although some firms operate without routing data. Other variations reflect different ways to suggest, report, and coordinate production activities (such as lean manufacturing environments), or make-to-order environments requiring linkage between production orders and sales orders. This argues for a contingency approach to modeling and managing production activity.

A production order represents the set of activities to produce an item. Differing types of production orders are used to model different types of production activities. This chapter starts with the basic structure and life cycle for a production order and an explanation of production order types. It explains the variations for reporting production activities and the primary tools for coordinating manufacturing. It also includes case studies of several manufacturing environments.

Production Orders

A production order provides one of the primary coordination tools for scheduling and reporting production activity. Effective use of a production order requires an understanding of product structure information such as item planning data, bills, and routings. Chapter 3 described this information for a manufac-tured item. Further explanation builds on this foundation.

Production Order Structure and Life Cycle

The basic structure of a production order consists of header and line item in-formation. As a reflection of this basic structure, the production order number and line number uniquely identify a scheduled receipt. A production order and its line items can be entered manually or generated automatically, as explained more fully in the next section concerning production order types and creation methods. Each line item specifies a material item, order quantity, due date, and the manufacturing location. Each line item can have an order-dependent bill and routing that drive material and capacity requirements.

The life cycle of a production order consists of several steps represented by an order status, as explained below.

* *Planned.* A planned production order is typically created from a sug-gested action message so that capacity requirements can be calculated. It can also be manually entered. However, planning calculations delete planned production orders and create a new set of suggested action messages.

* *Firm-Planned.* A firm-planned production order is typically created to indicate scheduling decisions over the near-term time horizon. Sched-uling decisions and the near-term horizon reflect several consider-ations, such as an item's cumulative manufacturing lead-time and constraints on material and capacity. As a result of constraints in some cases, the user may assign a different bill or routing version to the or-der or modify the order-dependent bill and routing.

* *Released.* A released status indicates an authorization to initiate and re-port activities for all line items. The released status is required to initi-ate several related actions, such as generating a suggested purchase for each outside operation and generating a warehouse document for pick-ing components. It can also trigger auto-deduction of forward-flushed components and work center time.

   Production activity is reported against an individual line item, such as reporting material consumption, unit completions by operation, and parent item completions. Completion quantities can exceed the order quantity. A production order may be temporarily placed on hold (blocked) to prevent further reporting, but the hold status does not af-fect planning calculations. The status of individual activities related to a released production order can also be identified. For example, a rout-ing operation can be designated as finished.

◆ *Finished.* A finished status must be assigned to indicate all production activity has been reported for all line items. The system provides a warning when it detects any activity still unreported. The finished status prevents further reporting and the order cannot be reopened. Changing to a finished status can trigger auto-deduction of backward-flushed components and work center time. The system calculates variances and retains a historical record for each finished order.

Production order status can be updated manually for a single order or automatically for a user-defined set of multiple orders. For example, the planner may update next week's schedule of firm-planned orders to a released status, or change status to finished for a group of released orders.

A numbering policy determines whether the same production order number apples to each order status (planned, firm-planned, and released) or a different order number applies to each status.

Production Order Types and Creation Methods

Modeling different types of production activities sometimes requires different types of production orders. A production order typically represents the set of production activities to build a single item, and the item defines the source of information for what needs to be done. Some types of production activities require linkage to the source of sales order demand, for example, or involve a single production process that generates multiple items reflecting a family of coproducts. These two examples involve designating the source of information for what needs to be done, such as the sales order demand or the family of coproduct items. Another example involves closely linking production activities to build a make-to-order product comprised of make-to-order components. Multiple linked production orders are required to represent this multilevel product structure. These examples argue for different types of production orders.

The types of production orders can be characterized by the source of information (termed *source type*) for its line items, the method for creating the order, and the manufacturing policy for an item and its components. These three factors affect the behavior and usage of a production order, especially the automatic creation of line items. It means that header information provides more than default values. The header information provides the basis for initially creating line items and for subsequently mass-updating line items. For example, the line items can be mass updated by changes in header information about the order quantity, due date, and/or manufacturing location.

The combinations of source type, manufacturing policy, and creation method are displayed in Figure 8.1 in terms of their impact on line item creation. The

Source Type	Key Factors		Method for Creating Production Order			
	Manufacturing Policy for Item		Manually Entered	System-Generated from Suggested Action Message	Generated from Sales Order	
	Parent	"Make" Component			Unrelated Lines	Related Lines (Project Order)
Manual Entry	N/A	N/A	Define 1+ Lines	N/A		
Item	MTS	N/A	Creates 1 Line		Creates 1 Production Order per SO Line	N/A
	MTO	MTS				
		MTO		Creates Extra Line	Creates Extra Line On Prod Order	
Sales Order	MTS	N/A	Creates 1 Line per SO Line	N/A		Creates 1 Line per SO Line
	MTO	MTS				
		MTO	Creates Extra Line			Creates Extra Line
Family of Items	MTS	N/A	Creates 1 Line per Family Member	N/A		
	MTO	MTS				
		MTO	Creates Extra Line			

Figure 8.1   Production Order Types and Creation Methods: Impact on Creating Line Items

source type for a production order provides an organizing focus for further explanation.

Production order header information can be manually entered, and line item information can then be manually entered or created automatically based on header information. Automatic creation of line items depends on the source type for the production order.

Manual Entry of Line Items   A *blank* source type indicates a manually entered production order that requires manual entry of line items. After entering one or more line items, the user can manually or automatically create each item's order-dependent bill and routing. Automatic creation requires a user-initiated process termed *refresh production order*, using the options to regenerate just the order-dependent bill and routing information. Using the option to calculate lines (for the refresh process) would delete the manually entered lines, since a specified source does not exist.

A line item can also be manually added to any production order. The order-dependent bill and routing can then be manually entered for the additional line or created automatically using the refresh process as described above.

Parent Item as the Source of Line Item Information   A manually entered production order can specify header information about a parent item. It also specifies the order quantity, due date, and manufacturing location. This is termed a *source item,* and the parent item can be a manufactured or purchased product. This header information can be used to automatically create the line item(s) and order-dependent bill/routing information. Automatic creation requires the refresh process using the options to also regenerate the line items.

With a manually entered production order, the refresh process creates a single-line order for a purchased or manufactured item. It creates an extra line for each make-to-order component of a make-to-order manufactured item. Each extra line item is linked to its parent line item, thereby reflecting the parent's multilevel product structure using multiple linked orders. The system uses the bill information to calculate appropriate quantities as well as start/end dates for these lower-level components. The refresh process may be repeated to reflect changes to header or bill information.

Production orders with an item source are typically generated from suggested action messages for manufactured items. When carrying out the suggested action, the system creates a production order header specifying the item, order quantity, due date, and manufacturing location. The suggested manufacturing location reflects demands. The suggested order quantity and date reflect the item's reordering policy, such as lot-for-lot or order-driven. As described above, a make-to-order manufacturing policy for an item and its components results in additional line items to represent the multilevel product structure.

Production orders with an item source can also be generated directly from a sales order, as shown in Figure 8.1. A user-initiated function generates a separate production order corresponding to each sales order line for a manufactured item. This approach reflects unrelated sales order line items for production purposes. With related line items, the user can alternatively create a multiline production order linked to the sales order. The related line items represent a single project for the sales order, and the production order is termed a *project order*. In this case, the production order has a source type of sales order (rather than item).

Sales Order as the Source of Line Item Information   A production order can be manually created with a sales order as the source type. The refresh process creates a production order with line items that correspond to each sales order line for a manufactured item. In the case of a multiline sales order, the line items are viewed as related, and the multiline production order represents a single project for the sales order. This approach allows the user to manually assign the same order number and provides greater visibility on the linkage between the production order and sales order.

A production order with a sales order source can also be generated directly from a sales order. As described above, the order entry person must choose to create a project order.

Family of Items as a Source of Line Item Information   A production order for a family of items provides one approach for handling coproducts or items produced simultaneously by a shared manufacturing process. Common examples include a molding, cutting, slitting, or sorting process, or an oven or sterilization process for a batch of different items. This approach avoids multiple production orders to model a single manufacturing process. The multiple items are defined as members of a user-defined family, with a master routing assigned to the family that identifies the common process. The production order header specifies the family, and the refresh process creates multiple line items with one line per family member. Line items can be added or deleted, and quantities changed, to reflect expected output. The order-dependent routing for each line item reflects the master routing assigned to the family (rather than each item's routing). The system supports a simplified approach to reporting production activities, with reporting of material consumption and work center time against the entire order while reporting actual output against individual line items.

Production Order Considerations

The basic production order information defines an item, quantity, due date, and manufacturing location. Additional considerations include the order-dependent bill and routing, text, reservations, and order statistics.

Order-Related Text   Most of the explanatory text for a production order is defined by bill of material and routing information. For example, the routing defines operation sequences and descriptions while the bill defines each operation's required material. Additional text can be specified as comments for the order header.

Order-Dependent Bill   A production order line item identifies the master bill (and bill version if applicable) acting as the source of the order-dependent bill. It defaults from the item's planning data and can be overridden. The components initially reflect those in effect as of the order due date. Component information can be manually changed, such as indicating a material substitution. Other changes include a component's flushing method, routing link code, or scrap percentage. The order-dependent bill defines the basis for a printed pick list or components in a pick document. It can be deleted and recreated by the refresh process using the option to calculate needed components.

Order-Dependent Routing   The definition of an order-dependent routing and bill are similar. A production order line item identifies the master routing (and routing version if applicable) acting as the source of the order-dependent routing. It typically defaults from the item's planning data and can be overridden. Routing operation information can be manually changed, such as indicating an alternate operation or time requirement. Other changes include the operation description, flushing method, routing link code, or scrap percentage. The order-dependent routing defines the basis for a printed shop traveler. It can be deleted and recreated by the refresh process using the option to calculate routing.

The Manufacturing Location for a Production Order and the Location for Its Components   The manufacturing location for a production order is specified for each line item and normally reflects the header information. The location for component requirements is normally the same as the parent item (on the line item), although it can be overridden in the order-dependent bill. In some cases, a different location for components is explicitly identified in the SKU planning data. For example, a location representing a service parts area may build an item that requires components from the manufacturing location.

Production Order Lead-Time and Manual Scheduling   Production lead-time represents one time element in the activities for a production order line item. As shown in Figure 8.2, the other time elements include picking components and putting away output (termed outbound and inbound warehouse handling time), and possibly safety lead-time for the manufactured item.

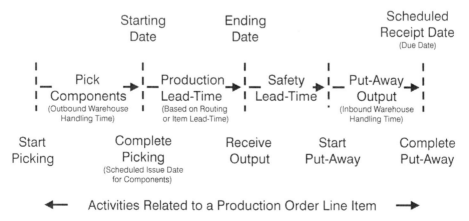

Figure 8.2   Critical Dates and Lead-Time Elements for a Production Order

The system calculates production lead-time for a production order line based on the order-dependent routing (if available) or the item's lead-time (if routing data is unavailable). Backward scheduling logic calculates a starting date and ending date from a due date. When the user changes one date, the system automatically updates the other date. Flagging an operation in the order-dependent routing as manually scheduled disables this automatic update.

Safety lead-time is handled slightly differently for a multiline production order with linkage between lines. This type of order represents a make-to-order manufactured item with make-to-order components. The system ignores an item's safety lead-time since it assumes make-to-order components are immediately used in the next level.

Guidelines for Refreshing a Production Order The refresh process provides one approach for manually updating production order information, with options about regenerating line items and the order-dependent bills or routings. The refresh process can only be performed prior to entering ledger entries for the order.

Line item regeneration is typically used after changing the item source, order quantity, due date, or manufacturing location in the header. With a make-to-order product, for example, regeneration can identify different line items when changes in the master bill affect make-to-order components. With a sales order source, for example, regeneration can identify different line items after changes to the sales order.

Manual changes to the order-dependent bill and/or routing will be overridden by the refresh process unless the user de-selects these options. The refresh process also provides an option for forward or backward scheduling; this is a user preference. The replan process (described next) may be used when you only require an updated schedule.

Guidelines for Replanning a Production Order The replan process provides one approach for manually scheduling a single production order, with an option about the scheduling impact. Scheduling can impact just the single order, the order's first-level components, or all levels of components. Scheduling can be forward or backward.

Reserving Components for a Production Order A component's inventory can be reserved for a production order line item. The user can manually specify the reserved material or use automatic reservations. Reservations can be made for lot- and serial-traced material as well as non-traced material.

Reserving the Expected Output of a Production Order for a Sales Order   The expected output for a production order line item can be reserved for a sales order. This approach to a reservation avoids waiting until output has been received into inventory.

Creating a Production Order via Copying an Existing Order

The copy feature can be used to create production order line items or the entire order from an existing order. When copying just the line items, the new line items are incrementally added and assigned a due date and manufacturing location based on header information. Copying an entire order with its header information replaces the header information and line items. After copying, the refresh process can create an order-dependent bill and routing for each existing line item, or completely regenerate line items based on header information.

Component Forecast Consumption by Production Orders

A production order line consumes the item's component forecast (if specified) to avoid doubled-up requirements. The line item's due date dictates forecast consumption within an implied forecast period.

Statistics for a Production Order   The statistics provide a cost summary of standard, expected, and actual costs to-date for all line items on a production order. The expected costs reflect the order-dependent bill and routing for each line item. A breakdown by cost element identifies costs related to material, capacity and capacity overhead (internal operations), subcontracts (outside operations), and manufacturing overhead (reflecting indirect costs for a parent item).

Using a Simulated Production Order for a One-Time Product

A simulated production order provides one approach to define and cost a one-time product, such as an engineering prototype item or a quote for a custom item. A what-if analysis can also assess the impact of producing the simulated order. A simulated production order can be copied or converted to a normal (or regular) production order. There are several key differences between the two types of production orders

Defining and Costing a Simulated Order   A one-time product can be defined using one or more line items. A line item provides the starting point for defining an order-dependent bill and routing, with an immediate calculation of expected costs. The line items can be automatically created (based on the source type), manually added, or both. Line items can also be copied from other production orders. With manual additions, the line item often identifies a newly created item number or an existing item number for a previously defined product. A line item could also specify a generic item number that provides the basis for defining an order-dependent bill. The generic item defines the basis for a unit of measure, item tracking policies, general ledger account numbers, planner responsibility, and other item attributes

Expected costs for the simulated order reflect the order-dependent bill and routing for each line item.

Differences between a Simulated and Regular Production Order   A simulated production order shares many similarities to a regular production order, such as the order structure, the creation of line items based on source type, and the maintenance of the order-dependent bill and routing for each line item. However, there are several major differences.

- ◆ *Ignored by Planning Calculations.* The line items are not considered scheduled receipts, and requirements for material and capacity are ignored. This allows a simulated order to be used for cost estimating or order preparation purposes only.

- ◆ *Sales Quote as a Source Type.* A sales quote (rather than a sales order) can be specified as the source type for the production order.

Once a simulated production order has been defined, further processing steps to build the one-time product(s) reflect two major variations.

- ◆ *Build the One-Time Product Without a Sales Order.* The simulated production order can be converted or copied to a production order. Planning calculations can then coordinate production activities and material requirements. If a sales order is subsequently entered for the one-time product, the existing production order can be reserved for the sales order.

- ◆ *Build the One-Time Product for a Sales Order.* The sales order can be generated or copied from the sales quote, or it may be manually entered. In addition, the simulated production order must be converted (or copied) to a production order, and the production order reserved for the sales order.

What-if Analysis for Building a Simulated Production Order
To perform a what-if analysis, a firm planned production order must be created (using a copy of the simulated production order) so the planning calculations recognize the material and capacity requirements. This also supports calculation

of a projected completion date based on forward scheduling logic. The firm planned order can then be deleted after performing the what-if analysis.

Reporting and Tracking Production Activities

Production orders involve reporting of several types of activities. These include component material consumption, routing operation time and unit completions, and production order output of completed items. Auto-deduction can minimize reporting for material consumption and operation time. The activities can be reported manually or automatically through a data collection system.

Reporting Material Component Usage

Component materials can be manually issued or auto-deducted based on their flushing method. Manual issues are typically initiated based on a printed pick list identifying the remaining component quantities that need to be issued to a production order. Actual component usage can be recorded on the Consumption Journal window. As a short-cut approach to recording information, the window displays all components for a specified production order (using the calculate consumption function), so that the user can easily review and post many transactions. Over- and underconsumption can also be recorded before the order status is changed to finished.

A pick document provides an alternative approach to initiate manual issues and report actual component usage for a production order. It identifies required component quantities for one production order. It can be created from the production order, or the production order subsequently associated with a pick document. Actual quantities picked are reported against the pick document, and posting the pick document reduces the component inventory balances.

Auto-deduction of components depends on their flushing method in the order-dependent bill and linkage to routing operations. Chapter 3 described flushing methods for reporting material usage. Over- and underconsumption is manually reported on the Consumption Journal window.

Reporting for an Internal Routing Operation

Reporting for an internal operation involves unit completions and/or operation time.

- ◆ *Reporting Unit Completions by Operation.* Units completed at an operation can be designated as good or scrapped, with an optional scrap reason code. The unit completions provide one measure of progress against the routing. They can trigger auto-deduction of back-flushed material linked to the operation. They can also trigger auto-deduction of operation time for a back-flushed work center.

Reporting unit completions for the last operation has special significance. The good unit completions indicate the output of the production order, and a location and bin must be specified for the received inventory. Additional information may need to be recorded about lot and serial numbers based on the item tracking policies for the parent item.

♦ *Reporting Operation Time.* Actual time reported for an operation reflects the work center time (and costs) rather than individual employee time (and labor rate). The actual time provides feedback for updating estimated times, and a measure of progress against the routing. The operation's remaining time is used in work center load analysis and production scheduling. An operation can be designated as finished so that the load analysis and production schedules ignore the operation's remaining time.

Unit completions and operation times are reported on the Output Journal window. As a short-cut to recording information, the window displays all internal routing operations for specified production orders (using the explode routing function) so that only units and/or time must be entered. Each routing operation is displayed as a separate line item, and posting updates all line items.

Auto-deduction of operation time depends on its flushing method, defined in the order-dependent routing. Chapter 3 described flushing methods for reporting operation time. Over- and underreporting of operation time is identified on the Output Journal window.

Reporting for an Outside Operation

An outside operation involves two streams of supply chain activities: one for the production order operation and a second for its related purchase order. The purchase order receipt provides reporting for an outside operation. Actual subcontract costs are updated for the production order based on the purchase price and quantity invoiced. No additional reporting is necessary for the production order unless the outside operation is the last operation in the routing (which requires reporting of the production order output).

Reporting Output of a Production Order

Output of a production order has several synonyms, such as work order receipts and parent item completions. The system provides two approaches for reporting output—one with routing data and one without—on the Output Journal window. With routing data, the good unit completions for the last operation define the output quantity. Without routing data, the parent item completions define output quantity (and operation information is not relevant).

Tracking Production Order Status

Production order status can be tracked in several ways. An order's statistics summarize actual costs expended to date in comparison to expected and standard costs. Progress against routing operations can be tracked in terms of unit completions or operation time or both, and a routing operation can also be flagged as finished. A comparison between order quantity and output quantity reported to date also provides a measure of production order status. The production order status should be changed from released to finished when all activities have been reported.

Coordinating and Executing Production Activities

A firm's game plans for saleable products provide the primary driver of production activities. The primary coordination tools for a manufacturing environment consist of a planning worksheet and production orders, plus work center load analysis and schedules when routing data has been defined.

Planning Worksheet and Suggested Action Messages

A planning worksheet identifies suggested action messages about production orders as well as purchase orders and transfer orders. Many manufacturing firms use just a planning worksheet, while others prefer to separate coordination of manufactured and purchased items with two types of worksheets—a planning worksheet and a requisition worksheet.[1] The suggested action messages can be analyzed, changed, and automatically implemented. The planning worksheet also provides the starting point for execution of planning calculations.

The planning worksheet can have multiple versions identified by a user-defined template name, just like the requisition worksheet. The use of different template names provides the ability to segment messages, as discussed below.

Execution of Planning Calculations
The user initiates execution of planning calculations from the planning worksheet. The planning calcula-

---

[1] The system uses three types of worksheets—a planning worksheet, a requisition worksheet, and a subcontracting worksheet—for coordinating supply chain activities.

tions can be performed on a regeneration or net-change basis; they calculate material and capacity requirements. They require a specified planning horizon and an order date (typically today's date). They are typically executed for all items, but they can be executed for a subset of items based on item number, location, or other filter.

Some firms prefer a two-phased approach to planning calculations. The first phase focuses on items (termed *MPS items*) with independent demands such as sales orders or forecast; the second phase focuses on all other items (termed *MRP items*).[2] The system determines whether an item is designated as an MPS or MRP item based on the presence of independent demand. With a two-phase approach, realistic schedules can be firmed up for MPS items before calculations are performed for MRP items. Most firms use the simpler one-phase approach.

In some situations, items may require immediate notification of suggested action messages without executing the planning calculations. These items have changes to their supplies or demands, such as changes to a sales order that must be communicated immediately. A user-initiated function gets and displays these action messages on the planning worksheet.

Suggested Action Messages   Suggested action messages are displayed on the version (or template name) of the planning worksheet that acted as the starting point for executing the planning calculations. The displayed messages reflect the entire planning horizon, all types of orders (purchase orders, production orders, and transfer orders), and five types of messages (new order, cancel order, reschedule order, change quantity, and reschedule and change quantity).

Segmenting Messages on the Planning Worksheet   Action messages may be segmented into subsets to support more effective coordination efforts. For example, a version (template name) of the planning worksheet can display a subset of action messages generated by planning calculations. Planning calculations must be initiated from the desired template name using a filter for the calculations such as a location. Using the location as a filter, planning calculations generate the location's suggested action messages on the template name.

---

[2] A master production schedule (MPS) typically represents the highest possible stocking level within a product structure and the level for defining forecasted demand to drive replenishment.

There are other examples of segmenting messages. Suggested action messages for purchase orders can be copied to the requisition worksheet (for a specified template name) or to another template name for the planning worksheet. In addition, situations requiring immediate attention (after a changed supply or demand) may be displayed on a separate template name that serves as the starting point for getting the action messages.

Filtering and Analyzing Messages   Messages can be filtered by planner responsibility with additional filters to focus attention on the subset of critical actions. For example, a filter regarding planner responsibility can be based on the Product Group Code or General Product Posting Group. Additional filters for identifying critical messages include the following examples.

- Messages for new production orders can be filtered and sorted based on order start date to focus attention on near-term actions. Special attention is required for suggested production with an order start date or due date before today's date.

- Messages for existing production orders can be filtered by starting or ending date, with special attention required when the due date is before today's date.

- Messages for purchase orders can be filtered by vendor and date information, such as identifying needed action for new purchases based on order start date. Grouping messages by vendor provides a convenient basis for communicating with each vendor.

Suggested action messages for production orders often require analysis to understand the rationale behind the suggestion or to assess the situation in more detail. For example, the user may need to review information about the item's supply/demand schedule, order-dependent bill and routing, or planning data. Analysis of a message concerning a production order can lead to one or more actions that can be implemented from the planning worksheet. Examples of taking action include:

- Changing and refreshing a production order. Changes to order quantity and due date, or assigning a different version of the master or routing, require a refresh process for the production order.

- Manually scheduling an existing production order. A production order can be manually scheduled when an operation in the order-dependent routing has been flagged as manually scheduled.

- Reserving component material.

- ◆ Inflexibility to make change. An existing production order line item can be flagged as having no planning flexibility, thereby suppressing further suggested action messages.

The ability to suppress unnecessary action messages makes the planning worksheet a better communication tool. For example, messages about rescheduling slightly later or changing quantity to slightly less can be suppressed using manufacturing setup policies about message dampeners.

Implementing Suggested Action Messages Messages can be automatically implemented based on the *accept action message* flag and the user-initiated process to carry out action messages. In many cases, suggested messages further out in the planning horizon should be deleted or not accepted to avoid inadvertent implementation. For example, creating production orders and purchase orders prematurely can lead to unnecessary rescheduling messages.

Implementation of suggested messages can be performed for all types of orders or just a selected type such as production orders. Implementation also supports copying the suggestions for purchase orders and transfer orders to the requisition worksheet (for a specified template name). The suggested action messages for new production orders are typically accepted and carried out to create planned orders so that capacity requirements can be generated. The next planning calculation run deletes the planned orders.

Subcontracting Worksheet for Outside Operations

Some manufacturing environments involve purchases of outside operations. The subcontracting worksheet displays suggestions for new purchases of outside operations for released production orders. It also provides the only method to create a purchase order for an outside operation. Chapter 6 described use of the subcontracting worksheet.

Capacity Planning and Load Analysis

The production order routing data provides the basis for analyzing work center loads to identify overloaded periods. Period size can be monthly, weekly, or daily, representing the range of aggregate to detailed analysis. The load analysis provides drill-down to the production order operations, so that load adjustment decisions can be made. Aggregate load analysis can also be viewed for a work center group.

The load analysis for a capacity-constrained work center can also identify overloaded periods and production orders that will be completed late as a result of the finite scheduling viewpoint.

Production Schedules

The production order routing data provides the basis for creating a production schedule by work center. The production schedule identifies each production order's routing operations performed in the work center. It consists of the same information as the load analysis drill-down but is presented in a format more appropriate for communicating the needed action. Production schedules can be displayed in different formats, such as tabular, Gantt chart, and schedule board.

A production schedule in tabular format identifies work center operations in a priority sequence with the hottest operations listed first. The simplest sequencing rule is based on operation start (or end) date and time. Operation information includes the remaining units and time and the units completed. It may include other information that proves useful to the planner or production personnel, such as the prior and next operation, the expected operation scrap percentage, and the operation description. Much of the information may be identified on a production order traveler, thereby minimizing the need for including it in the production schedule. Changes in the production schedule must be reflected in updated information about the affected production orders and their order-dependent routings, but this becomes cumbersome. Other production schedule formats make it easier to update this information.

Gantt Chart Format for a Production Schedule

There are several variations of a Gantt chart format for a production schedule. A simplistic format displays time along the horizontal axis and rows corresponding to production orders. It displays each production order as a bar, where bar length reflects the order's starting and ending date/time. A drag-and-drop feature performs the equivalent of manual scheduling of a production order (without changing bar length). A graphic load analysis may be displayed along the horizontal axis (e.g., for a bottleneck work center) to highlight overloaded periods and the impact of manual scheduling. Information about the affected production order(s) can be automatically updated.

Another format displays each operation within a production order as a bar, where bar length reflects each operation's starting and ending date/time. The drag-and-drop feature performs the equivalent of manual scheduling for an operation, with corresponding impacts on preceding and succeeding operations in the order-dependent routing. The rows in the Gantt chart display work centers so that an operation can be placed on a different work center. Information about the affected production order(s) and operations can be automatically updated.

The logic and capabilities underlying a Gantt chart production schedule can become very complex. For example, additional complexities include handling overlapping operations, concurrent operations, split operations, sequence-dependent setup times, and other advanced scheduling considerations. As a result of lean manufacturing practices the scheduling issues should become simpler, and a production schedule can be modeled as a simple schedule board.

Production Order Variances

The standard cost for a manufactured item provides the basis for variance analysis on a production order. Variances identify the differences between an item's standard cost and actual production order costs, and are summarized on the statistics window for a production order. Variances indicate potential problems in manufacturing an item, and diagnosis requires an understanding of how variances are calculated. Explanations here focus on a one-line production order, but they also apply to a multiline order.

The total variance for a given production order is graphically represented in Figure 8.3 as the distance between two lines representing the standard cost and actual costs for the order. The difference between the two lines consists of five types of variances. The figure also displays a separate line for an expected cost. These three lines provide the basis for an explanation of production order variances.

Standard Cost   The standard cost data for a manufactured item reflects company-wide information and a cost roll-up calculation as of a specified date. Chapter 3 explained standard cost roll-up calculations. An item's costs are segmented into material, capacity, capacity overhead, subcontracted, and manufacturing overhead. These cost elements provide the baseline for calculating the five types of variances.

Expected Cost   The expected costs for a production order reflect information in the order-dependent bill and routing. This information initially reflects the master bill and routing (and versions if applicable) assigned to the production order line item. Manual changes to this information typically represent substitute materials and/or alternate operations. The Production Order Statistics window displays the differences between expected costs and standard costs, but these are not considered variances from an accounting viewpoint.

Actual Costs   Actual costs for a production order reflect the reporting of production activities and the costs at transaction time. Differences between actual costs and standard cost can be segmented into five variances, and the basis for each variance differs. The typical basis for each variance is shown in Figure 8.3 and described below.

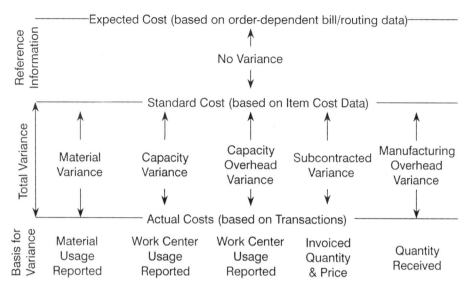

Figure 8.3   Production Order Variances

- *Material Variance.* Actual costs are based on reported material usage, so that variances indicate differences with information used to calculate the item's standard cost for material. This typically stems from over- or underreporting component quantity usage, or the component's SKU cost differs from the cost used in roll-up calculations.

- *Capacity Variance.* The reported capacity usage for an internal operation differs from that used to calculate the item's standard cost for capacity. A capacity variance is typically caused by over- or underreporting of time for an internal operation. Other causes include a production order quantity that differs from the parent item's accounting lot size since this affects the amortization of setup and fixed scrap amounts.

- *Capacity Overhead Variance.* The same explanation for capacity variance applies to a capacity overhead variance, where an internal work center has overhead costs.

- *Subcontracted Variance.* The invoiced quantity and/or price for an outside operation differs from that used to calculate the item's standard costs. Each outside operation typically has a specified unit cost in the routing information

- *Manufacturing Overhead Variance.* The parent item's received quantity differs from the production order quantity, which leads to differences in the incurred manufacturing overhead costs.

The general ledger is updated with variances for finished production orders after running the batch process to Adjust Cost-Item Entries. The value entries for the finished production order and for the parent item provide a transaction audit trail identifying each calculated variance.

The statistics window for a multiline production order summarizes standard, expected, and actual costs for all line items. However, the system retains information about variances related to each line item and displays it in the value entries for the finished production order.

Case Studies

Case #42: Planner Action Messages
The All-and-Anything company wanted to improve coordination of manufacturing activities by enhancing suggested planner action messages. Building on the concept of planner responsibility assigned to items and production order line items, they extended the scope of suggested action messages on the planning worksheet. Additional message types included follow-up on past-due receipt, review an order placed on hold, review an existing order affected by changes to the master bill or routing, and review an item when its primary source is changed to production. Message filters were also defined for various message types.[3]

Case #43: Production Order Variances
The cost accountant at the All-and-Anything company required several customizations to improve the usefulness of information about variances. For example, the costs for purchased material were segmented into material and material-related overhead cost elements, and the cost of sales was segmented into each cost element for posting to the general ledger. Additional variances were calculated for each production order, including variances between expected and standard costs, and variances related to issued components not on the order-dependent bill. This supported a better comparison between standard costs plus variances against actual costs. The cost accountant also required several reports to understand and analyze production order variances. One report provided a detailed breakdown (by component and operation) of standard versus actual costs to fully understand the cause of production order variances. Another report provided a historical analysis of each production order's variances by parent item, component, and work center.

---

[3] See *Maximizing Your ERP System* for further explanation of planner responsibility (pp. 116–117, 285) and types of planner action messages (pp. 290–292).

Case #44: Regulated Environment for Process Manufacturing

The Batch Process company produced a pharmaceutical product with stringent quality criteria concerning compliance with regulations and requirements for a validation audit. Starting with various lot-controlled ingredients, a batch is mixed, made into tablets, and then packaged in a bottle with a label. Each batch requires a unique lot number. Tablets are treated as phantoms since production flows from the tablet machine immediately into packaging.

The quality criteria in this regulated environment impact system usage in several ways. Systems security plays a larger role, such as authorized access to update information about bills, lots, inventory dispositions, and transaction audit trails. It requires strict label control, conditional releases of lot-traced material, and lot genealogy for historical analysis purposes (see Case #37 in Chapter 7).

Case #45: Customer-Supplied Material

The Equipment company occasionally used customer-supplied material in production processes. They required identification of component requirements in the bill, visibility of scheduled receipts, a receiving process, and material tracking for customer-supplied material. The item number for each customer-supplied component represented a unique item and was valued at zero cost.

Case #46: Advanced Planning and Scheduling (APS) Integration for a Fabricated Product

The Fabricated Products company required APS capabilities to minimize setups and avoid additional equipment purchases for its line of extruded plastic products. Multiple extrusion machines produced plastic pipes of varying diameters and colors. Scheduling considerations included sequence-dependent setup time (based on diameter and color), machine capabilities for handling different products, machine-specific run rates, and secondary resources of tooling and skilled operators. To integrate APS capabilities, the routing data was extended to specify a work center (the resource group) and a machine (the preferred resource) for an operation; operation attributes such as setup matrices for handling sequence-dependent setup times; and machine attributes such as resource type. The APS capabilities were also used to support capable-to-promise logic.[4]

---

[4] See *Maximizing Your ERP System* for further explanation of APS integration, including a summary of APS logic and the theory of constraints (pp. 30–34), resource types and resource groups (pp. 92–97), operation attributes (pp. 106–108), and using APS for capable-to-promise logic (pp.197–198).

Executive Summary

Production represents the distinctive competency of most manufacturers. A separate functional area termed production activity control is typically responsible for coordinating production activities. Modeling different types of production activities often requires different types of production orders. A production order typically represents the set of production activities to build a single item, and the item defines the source of information for what needs to be done. Some types of production activities require linkage to the source of sales order demand, so that the sales order defines the source of information for what needs to be done. In some cases, a simulated production order is created to define and cost a one-time product, and it can be converted to a production order. Several considerations apply to production orders, such as the order-dependent bill and routing, the production order lead-time, and reserving components for a production order. A production order can have a status of planned, firm-planned, or released. For a released production order, production activities can be reported for material usage, internal and external operations, and output of completed items. Coordination of production activities is based on production schedules by work center (if routing data is defined) and suggested action messages generated by planning calculations. Production order variances are calculated for a finished production order. The case studies highlighted variations in manufacturing environments, such as highly regulated operations and integration with advanced planning and scheduling (APS) capabilities.

Chapter 9

Multisite Operations

Many small to midsize businesses involved in manufacturing and distribution have multiple locations with inventory. Operations with multiple locations serve different purposes. A location may reflect proximity to suppliers or customers, transportation or production cost considerations, or availability of raw materials and human resources. There may be political, technological, or competitive considerations for multiple locations, or a location may represent an acquisition.

There are wide variations in the system requirements to support a multisite operation. The basic variations reflect requirements for material coordination between locations and how locations are grouped into companies (or financial entities). One company may have multiple locations, for example, or the locations may be grouped into different financial entities. The locations within a company may operate autonomously with no coordination requirements, or they may represent a vertically integrated supply chain with coordinated material flows between sites. Coordination typically requires transfer orders to communicate needed shipments (at the transfer-from location) and expected receipts (at the transfer-to location). Examples of multisite operations with higher coordination requirements include a distribution network, a remote warehouse, space within a contract warehouse, a customer location (for stocking material prior to customer usage), a subcontract vendor location (for stocking supplied components and/or the completed parent), a customer service center, and delivery vans. A separate service parts inventory (with separate replenishment policies) within a manufacturing company also represents a separate inventory location with coordination requirements.

This chapter covers how to handle the major variations in multisite operations, starting with the definition of location information. It reviews how transfer orders coordinate material movement between locations. Finally, it covers several scenarios that illustrate variations in multisite operations.

Use of Location Information for a Company with Multiple Sites

A location must be defined for each physical facility in which the company stocks inventory. In addition, the use of transfer orders requires definition of in-transit locations and a transportation lead-time matrix. The use of location codes has several system implications for a multisite company. Chapter 2 summarized the implications for a single-site company.

In-Transit Locations for Transfer Orders   Additional in-transit locations must be defined to support transfer orders. A transfer order involves moving material into and out of an in-transit location. When defining a location for this purpose, it must be specifically flagged as an in-transit location. Bin locations and other warehouse management policies do not apply to an in-transit location. Most firms define two in-transit locations—one for internal logistics and one for external logistics—to help differentiate the transportation provider.

Transportation Lead-Time Matrix and Transfer Routes   Each combination of transfer-from and transfer-to locations requires definition of a transfer route in order to support transfer orders. A Transfer Route window provides a matrix of possible combinations. Each matrix cell defines a unique transfer route consisting of three characteristics: the in-transit site, default shipping agent, and service. Transportation lead-time reflects the lead-time assigned to a shipping agent's service (such as FedEx second day delivery). In this sense, the Transfer Route window defines a transportation lead-time matrix.

System Implications for a Multisite Company

The use of multiple locations has several system implications for setup, item master information, customer and sales order information, vendor and purchase order information, and forecasts.

- *Setup Information.* An inventory setup policy designates that a location code must be specified for all item-related transactions. A transportation lead-time matrix must be defined for handling transfers between locations.
- *Item Master Information.* The item master defines company-wide information and location-specific information, as previously explained in Chapters 2 and 3.
- *Customer and Sales Order Information.* The preferred ship-from location can be designated for each customer and customer ship-to address; a blank indicates no preference. The preferred ship-from location acts

as a default on all sales documents. Each sales order line item, for example, can then designate the desired ship-from location.

◆ *Vendor and Purchase Order Information.* The preferred ship-to location can be designated for each vendor and vendor ship-from address; a blank indicates no preference. The preferred ship-to location acts as a default on all purchase documents. Each purchase order line item, for example, can designate the desired ship-to location.

◆ *Forecasts.* A setup policy designates that forecasts must be location-specific. Forecasts can then be entered by location, and a set of forecast data includes estimated demands for multiple locations.

Transfer Orders

A transfer order supports the coordination and execution of supply chain activities for material flows between two locations. It communicates requirements for moving material from one location (the transfer-from location) to replenish inventory at another location (the transfer-to location) within the same company. It also provides the means to track movement of in-transit inventory. Alternatively, an inventory movement transaction (termed an *item reclassification journal*) can be used to report movement, especially when minimal transportation lead-time eliminates the need for tracking in-transit inventory.

The structure and life cycle of a transfer order serve as a starting point for further explanation about transfer order considerations and how to report shipments and receipts.

Structure and Life Cycle of a Transfer Order

The basic structure of a transfer order consists of header and line item information. The transfer order header identifies the two sites involved (the transfer-from and transfer-to locations), and then provides a two-part header approach (one for each location) for defining additional header information. One part defines additional transfer-from information such as the shipment date and outbound handling time; the second part defines additional transfer-to information such as the receipt date and inbound handling time. This header information provides default values for line items and a mass update approach. For example, changing the receipt date in the header mass updates the receipt and shipment dates for all line items. The header also defines the in-transit location and the associated shipping agent, service, and transportation lead-time that apply to the entire transfer order.

As a reflection of this basic structure and the two-part header, the transfer order number and line number uniquely identify a scheduled shipment (at the transfer-from location) and a scheduled receipt (at the transfer-to location). The life cycle of a transfer order consists of several steps, with two steps represented by an order status as explained below.

- *Open.* An open status indicates the transfer order is being created. The order header has been created, and one or more line items can be defined. Information can be changed on an open transfer order, but items cannot be shipped until the status is changed to released.

- *Released.* A released status indicates the transfer order information has been completely entered and authorizes shipment for all line items. Information cannot be changed on a released transfer order, but it can be manually reopened to allow changes. A released order allows generation of documents (such as the pick and receipt documents) for warehouse management purposes.

Shipping activities at the transfer-from site are performed before receiving activities at the transfer-to site. That is, the transfer order lines are posted as shipped and subsequently posted as received. A line item is automatically flagged as completely shipped when the shipped quantity equals the order quantity; it is flagged as completely received when the received quantity equals the order quantity. The shipment cannot exceed the order quantity, and receipts cannot exceed the shipped quantity. The order is automatically deleted when order quantities for all line items have been posted as completely shipped and received. Historical information about a transfer order can be viewed on the windows for posted transfer shipments and posted transfer receipts.

Transfer Order Considerations

The basic transfer order information defines the item(s) to be transferred and the relevant locations. Many situations require additional considerations, such as order-related text and reserved material, as described below.

Manually Created vs. System-Suggested Transfer Orders

A transfer order can be created manually or in response to a suggested action message for a new transfer. Planning calculations suggest a new transfer based on SKU planning data about the preferred transfer-from location. Planning calculations reflect the normal transfer route between the two locations (which determines transportation lead-time) and the warehouse handling time at each location. Information about the transfer route—the shipping agent, service, and shipping time—can only be overridden after creating the transfer order.

The system creates a transfer order for each item and combination of locations, which means that the line items reflect only one item. Line items can also be manually added.

A manually created transfer order typically reflects an unplanned or emergency requirement to replenish inventory. The transfer order line items may be created for different items. In addition, the line items can be automatically created for all items within a bin at the transfer-from location (using the get bin contents function). This feature proves useful when moving many items from one location to another, especially when the items have been placed in a unique bin representing material to be shipped to a specific location.

Order-Related Text   Comments can be defined for a transfer order. Text can also be entered as a line item using the item description field and a null item number.

Shipment and Receipt Dates   The difference between a transfer order shipment and receipt date reflects the shipping time plus the warehouse handling time at each location. Changing the shipment date on a transfer order line item automatically updates the receipt date and vice versa. Changing the shipment or receipt date in the transfer order header automatically aligns all line items to the same dates.

Transfer Lead-Time and Capable-to-Promise Logic

Capable-to-promise (CTP) logic provides one approach to making sales order delivery promises for an out-of-stock item. CTP logic calculates a transfer item's earliest ship date based on the preferred transfer-from site and the related transportation lead-time and warehouse handling time.

Reserving Material for a Transfer Order   An SKU's inventory can be reserved for shipment on a transfer order line item. With a manual approach to reservations, the user can prompt a review of existing inventory and manually select inventory to be reserved.

Reporting a Transfer Order Shipment and Receipt

Shipping and receiving activities represent the completion of a transfer order, and different approaches can be taken to report these activities. The basic approach focuses on reporting shipping (and then receiving) activity against line items on an individual transfer order. In many cases, a printed version of the transfer order serves as a pick list and identifies the items' bin locations. It also serves as a turnaround document for recording actual quantities shipped, along with the actual bin locations and applicable lot or serial numbers. Actual shipment can then be entered on the Transfer Order window; the same window can be used to report receipts.

Other approaches can be used to report transfers that support requirements for coordinating warehouse management activities. These approaches use a separate pick document and/or shipment document to coordinate shipping activities at the transfer-from location, plus receipt and put-away documents at the transfer-to location. These documents were described in Chapter 7.

Coordinating Transfer Order Activities

A firm's game plans for saleable products provide the primary driver of transfer orders. Coordination of transfer orders to meet the game plans is accomplished by suggested action messages and warehouse management activities.

S&OP Game Plans in a Multisite Operation

The sales and operations planning process results in a game plan for each item and location. For stocked items, the S&OP game plan may be expressed in terms of an order-point replenishment method for each SKU. The game plan may also include forecasted demand, expressed as a sales forecast and/or component forecast by location. Sales orders for a given item and ship-from location consume the item's sales forecast for the location. The designated ship-from site may reflect sourcing rules such as the default ship-from location for a customer. In many cases, the ship-from site may reflect availability to meet delivery date requirements.

Some multisite operations require transfers to replenish inventory at a location. Suggested transfer orders reflect distribution requirements planning (DRP) logic built into the planning calculations.

Suggested Action Messages on the Planning or Requisition Worksheet

Suggested action messages about new and existing transfer orders can be viewed on the requisition worksheet or the planning worksheet. Use of these worksheets was previously described for purchase orders (Chapter 6) and production orders (Chapter 8), and the recommendations apply to transfer orders. Planning calculations generate the same type of messages for transfer orders, such as create a new order and reschedule an existing order. Action messages may be segmented, filtered, and sorted to support more effective coordination efforts such as viewing messages for a selected transfer-from and/or transfer-to location. Suggestions may also require analysis of an item's supply/demand information. Infeasible suggestions such as rescheduling a transfer order earlier should be flagged as having "no planning flexibility" to suppress further messages. Suggestions can be automatically implemented.

Suggestions for a new transfer order communicate the need to ship material. Rather than create a new transfer order to ship and receive material, some situations with minimal transportation time between locations (such as adjoining sites) often use an inventory move transaction.

Warehouse Management Activities Regarding Transfer Orders

Several different approaches can be used coordinate and report shipments and receipts. Coordination and reporting of shipping activities can be based on a printed pick list for each transfer order, a pick document, and/or a ship document. In a similar fashion, receiving activities can be based on use of the transfer order, a receipt document, and/or a put-away document. The advantages of using these documents were covered in Chapter 7.

Variations in Multisite Operations

Wide variations exist between companies with multiple locations. The following scenarios illustrate some of these variations.

Scenario #1: Autonomous Locations with Centralized Order Entry

Each location operates autonomously, with no material movement between locations. Company-wide information is defined for customers, sales prices, vendors, and items; SKU information is defined for each location. Sales orders can be taken for shipment from any location, with the ship-from location designated for each sales order line item. Approved vendors and purchase agreements apply to purchased materials at all locations. A centralized purchasing function coordinates delivery of common raw materials, with purchase order line items designating the ship-to locations. A centralized group handles accounting—such as receivables, payables, and general ledger—for all locations.

Scenario #2: Central Location Supplying Other Location(s)

The central location may represent a distribution center or a manufacturing plant. The other locations may represent a variety of situations, such as a remote finished goods warehouse, consigned inventory stocked at a customer site, or a separate service parts inventory. Transfer orders replenish inventory at the other locations based on SKU planning data.

Scenario #3: Inventory Stocked at a Subcontractor Location

Inventory stocked at a subcontractor location can represent three different cases. Purchased components can be shipped directly to the subcontractor, material components can be transferred to the subcontractor from another location, and the manufactured item (built via an outside operation) can be stocked at the subcontractor. The manufactured item has a master bill defining the supplied material and a master routing with the outside operation performed by the subcontractor.

Scenario #4: One Manufacturing Plant Building an Item for Another Plant

This scenario has two variations that can be labeled *transfer complete* and *subcontract*. In the transfer complete scenario, the parent item at the supplying plant is identified as manufactured (in the SKU planning data), while the same item at the consuming plant is identified as transfer (in the SKU planning data). The consuming plant does not return the completed item.

The subcontract scenario involves supplied material and a completed item that is returned to the supplying plant. The completed item is built at the consuming plant using the supplied material. At the consuming plant, the SKUs for supplied components are identified as transfer and the completed item's SKU is manufactured. At the supplying plant, the completed item's SKU is designated as transfer.

Scenario #5: One Manufacturing Plant Building Items Using Components from Another Location

Components are normally located at the same location as the production order for the parent item, but some multisite operations require an exception to this rule. Two examples will help clarify this exception. One example involves a manufacturing plant and a separate service parts location, where production orders in the service parts location use components stocked at the manufacturing plant. A second example involves a manufacturing plant with an adjoining raw material warehouse treated as a separate location; components for production orders are issued directly from the adjoining warehouse. These two examples could be modeled using the company-wide setup policy concerning the location of components, or by using the SKU's Components at Location field to indicate the alternate source of components. This enables planning calculations to correctly interpret requirements for replenishing inventory at the adjoining location.

Scenario #6: Multiple Manufacturing Plants that Build Different Items

The manufacturing plants have common raw materials but build different subassemblies and products identified by unique item numbers. Each of the manufactured items has a master bill and routing, where work centers for all locations are defined in the work center master. Requirements for raw materials are driven by production orders, where the production order location drives location-specific requirements for raw materials. The purchase order line items identify the ship-to locations for purchasing common raw materials.

Scenario #7: Multiple Manufacturing Plants that Build the Same Item

Two or more manufacturing plants build the exact same item, where the item may be a subassembly or finished good. The master bill provides a company-wide standard for component materials. The planning calculations correctly interpret component requirements based on the production order location (which reflects item demands for the location).

Some manufacturing environments require a different bill of material for building the exact same item at different locations; a company-wide standard does not apply. One solution approach employs different versions of the master bill for each location-specific bill. This represents an authorized recipe approach. Firm planned production orders can be used to specify location and the bill version to be used.

The authorized recipe concept also applies to different routings for building the exact same item at different locations. Different versions of the routing reflect location-specific work centers or processing times. Firm planned production orders can be used to specify location and the routing version to be used.

Scenario #8: Multisite Operations Segmented into Multiple Companies

The segmentation of multiple locations into different companies often reflects different countries for the locations. Each country has unique accounting requirements that can be better served by a separate company within the database or by a country-specific version of Microsoft Navision. A separate company has separate information about items, locations, customers, and vendors. Trading between two companies involves a customer-to-vendor relationship, and transfers between locations in different companies involve the use of purchase orders and sales orders. The Biztalk documents for purchase orders and sales orders can automate the required transaction processing.

Case Studies

Case #47: Centralized MPS   A diaper manufacturing company had several plants spread around the United States that produced the exact same items—different types of diapers—using the exact same equipment. Production volumes at each location reflected the local demand, but production was sometimes shifted between plants when one was overloaded. This required centralized master scheduling. Different versions of a master routing were defined that identified location-specific work centers, and firm-planned production orders for each location specified the correct routing version. A work center group was defined for these work centers to provide aggregate capacity planning and support centralized master scheduling.

Case #48: Multinational Food Products   A multinational food products manufacturer had multiple plants and distribution centers around the world. The manufacturing plants were located close to the source of raw materials, while the distribution centers were located close to the customers. Each location operated as a separate company, so that the transfers between locations were handled as a sales order shipment and purchase order receipt. The placement of purchase orders at a distribution center automatically created an associated sales order at the manufacturing plant. The sales order shipment (at the plant) automatically created a purchase order receipt (at the distribution center) into a bin location representing in-transit inventory.

Case #49: Food Bank Distributor   More than 100 autonomous food bank distributors use a customized version to handle unique requirements for inventory and financial management. This includes FIFO inventory handling rules with exceptions for product lot expiration dates, inventory repack and kitting, and donations management. It includes business logic for qualifiers about shoppers and agency orders (such as food kitchens), and support for grant usage and fund accounting. Each distributor operates as a stand-alone business entity with a separate copy of the software.[1]

Case #50: Offshore Sales Company   An equipment manufacturer had four plants spread around the United States that operated as autonomous companies. The firm's chief executive lived on a Caribbean island, which was also the location of an offshore company that processed sales orders for the manufacturing plants. A sales order was entered for a piece of equipment with

---

[1] See SecondHarvest.org for more information.

a drop-ship purchase order communicated to one of the four "vendors" that were the manufacturing plants. The company associated with each manufacturing plant had only one sold-to customer (the offshore company) and many bill-to customers (the firms that bought the equipment).

Executive Summary

There are wide variations in multisite operations. The basic variations reflect requirements for material coordination between locations and how locations are grouped into companies. A transfer order supports material coordination between two locations within the same company. Several scenarios illustrated variations in multisite operations. These scenarios included autonomous sites with centralized order entry and the use of multiple locations and transfer orders to handle a remote finished goods warehouse, consigned inventory stocked at a customer site, a separate service parts inventory, and material stocked at subcontractors. The scenarios also included inventory replenishment across a company's distribution network. The case studies provided further illustrations of multisite variations, such as centralized master scheduling and an offshore sales order company.

Chapter 10

Summary

The starting point of this book is that supply chain management requires effective use of an integrated ERP system. Its central theme focuses on using Microsoft Navision for managing supply chain activities in small to midsize manufacturers and distributors. Its target audience includes those individuals implementing or considering Microsoft Navision as their ERP system. The book addresses an overall understanding of how the system fits together to run a business, expressed in generally accepted terminology. This mental framework—in combination with hands-on experience and training courseware—can accelerate the learning process, and an overall understanding leads to more effective system usage.

Usage of any ERP system—including Microsoft Navision—is shaped by many design factors that make it easier (or harder) to learn and use. For example, consistency and symmetry in the user interface make an ERP system easier to learn and use. The same holds true for the consistency and symmetry in standardized functionality across integrated applications, and in extended functionality stemming from customizations and independently developed software. System functionality and e-commerce integration also shape usage in different manufacturing and distribution environments.

Many of the design factors related to Microsoft Navision have been covered in previous chapters. This final chapter summarizes the design factors shaping system usage and hopefully provides the capstone of an overall understanding about how the system fits together to run manufacturing and distribution businesses. The design factors are segmented into those related to the user interface, customization capabilities, and system usage in manufacturing and distribution environments. Additional design factors include those related to integration with e-commerce, relationship management, service management, and accounting applications.

Design Factors Related to the User Interface

The user interface within Microsoft Navision provides consistency across all windows that assist ease-of-learning and ease-of use. In addition, a graphical user interface supports user-defined work flows so that a user can select the desired step and access the relevant window. A few illustrations are provided below about the basic types of windows comprising the user interface.

Card vs. List Format   Records can be viewed individually in card format or all together in list format, where the list format works very much like a spreadsheet. Customer master data, for example, can be viewed and maintained in card format for a single customer or viewed in list format for all customers. Both formats support access to related information and forward/backward browsing. The card format often segments data into tabs, while records in a list format can be copied and pasted into a spreadsheet.

Some windows with header and line item information employ a combination of card format and list format. A sales order, for example, consists of header information in card format and line items in list format. The header information for all sales orders can be viewed in list format.

Find Capabilities   Find capabilities can be based on any string of embedded text in a record identifier (such as customer number) or its attributes.

Filtering and Sorting   A filter limits the displayed records based on values in one or more fields, with sorting based on any field. The user can browse forward and backward through the subset. Filtering logic includes equal to, different from, greater than, less than, intervals, and wild cards.

Drill-Down Analysis   The system supports several drill-down approaches, such as drill-down to the source transactions and drill-down to the details comprising a summarized value.

Design Factors Related to Customization Capabilities

Customizations range from the simple to the complex. Complex customizations typically entail significant changes to system functionality and logic. Simple customizations typically involve minor changes to the user interface and reports and do not impact system logic. Several tools support simple customizations as illustrated below.

Customizing Window Layout for the List Format   The list format allows an end-user to tailor window layout by selectively hiding, showing, and sorting fields via drag-and-drop. This provides a simple approach to customizing window layout and the system remembers each end-user's preferences. In addition, an end-user can view all available fields (and their values) in the table related to a record.

Customizing Window Layout for the Card Format

The card format can be changed with an easy-to-use forms designer, such as changes to field labels, to show or hide fields, and to rearrange fields on tabs.

Customizing Reports and Documents

The format and content of reports and documents (such as an invoice) can be customized using a report designer tool. The tool also supports export/import for exchanging spreadsheet data.

Customizing via Additional Fields

New fields can be added to tables with immediate visibility in list format windows and availability for customizing card formats and reports.

The object-oriented design also supports more complex customizations. Numerous case studies throughout the book illustrated some of these customizations.

Design Factors Shaping System Usage in Distribution Environments

Major factors shaping system usage include item definition, symmetry of sales and purchasing functionality, sales variations, symmetry of warehouse functionality, and the capabilities to model variations in multisite operations.

Item Definition

Item master information consists of company-wide and location-specific information. Company-wide information, for example, includes the item number, lot/serial tracking policies, and a costing method (such as standard cost or an actual costing method). Location-specific information includes the item's costs and replenishment method for each location. Non-stock items can be defined in the item master, as well as item variant codes to handle color/size variations of the same item.

Primary Engine for Coordinating Supply Chain Activities

Planning calculations synchronize supplies to meet demands and generate suggested action messages on worksheets. Replenishment logic within the planning calculations includes time-phased order point and DRP and MRP logic.

Symmetry of Sales and Purchasing Functionality Sales and purchasing both handle documents for quotes, blanket orders, orders, invoices, returns, and credit memos, with parallel approaches for handling cross-reference identifiers, prices and discounts, special charges, and order-related text. Symmetry is also apparent in the definition of customer and vendor information and the handling of special orders and drop shipments.

Variations in Sales Sales order line items can identify material items (including special orders, drop shipments, and kits of components) as well as resource time, special charges, and text. Pricing and discounting schemes can reflect product and customer groups, quantity breakpoints and date effectivities, and discounts based on total order value. Sales can be forecasted to drive purchasing requirements.

Symmetry of Warehouse Functionality for Inbound and Outbound Shipments The same functionality for handling outbound shipments applies to sales orders, transfer orders, and returns to vendor. Similar functionality for handling inbound shipments applies to purchase orders, transfer orders, and customer returns.

Variations in Warehousing Shipping activities can focus on individual orders or a pick document, while receiving activities can focus on individual orders or a receipt document and an optional put-away document. Put-away suggestions can optionally account for bin location considerations, such as location preferences and capacity constraints. Movement within a warehouse can reflect bin replenishment policies, such as replenishing bins from a bulk storage area.

Modeling Variations in Multisite Operations The system supports different types of multisite operations, including autonomous sites within a company and a distribution network with transfers between locations. Costs and replenishment methods can be defined by item and location, where the replenishment method can identify the preferred ship-from location (and transportation lead-time considerations) to model a distribution network. Transfer orders coordinate movement between locations. Sales order line items indicate the ship-from location, while purchase order line items indicate the ship-to location.

Design Factors Shaping System Usage in Manufacturing Environments

In addition to the above-mentioned factors for distribution environments, the major factors shaping system usage in manufacturing environments include the definition of product structure, variations in production strategy, and lean manufacturing practices.

Definition of Product Structure Information Master bills and master routings define product and process design, with optional bill and routing versions. Their identifiers are assigned to relevant manufactured items and specified on production orders. Planned engineering changes are identified using date effectivities for each bill and routing version; date effectivities can also be identified for material components. The master bill and routing information provide the basis for costing and planning calculations. Routing information is optional, and some firms coordinate production activities without it.

The order-dependent bill and routing for a production order initially reflect the assigned master bill and routing, and can be manually maintained to identify a custom configuration. The system models a multilevel custom product configuration using order-dependent bills and multiple linked production orders tied to the sales order.

Variations in Production Strategy Selling stocked product involves a make-to-stock production strategy, where sales forecasts typically drive end-item replenishment. A make-to-order production strategy often requires stocked components, where replenishment may be driven by component forecasts. The production order for a make-to-order product is typically linked to a sales order. A make-to-order product may have make-to-order components, so that multiple linked production orders are tied to the sales order. The linked production order(s) can be generated during sales order entry, by planning calculations, or by manual assignment.

Lean Manufacturing Practices Lean manufacturers often require auto-deduction of material and resources, bin replenishment of floor stock material, orderless reporting of production, and/or constraint-based scheduling of manufacturing cells.

Integration with Warehouse Management

Integrated warehouse management functionality is already included, thereby avoiding the need for a supplemental application. It supports both order-based and document-based approaches to warehouse management, and a natural growth path to more advanced functionality. For example, suggested put-aways can account for item characteristics (such as weight or cold storage requirements) as well as bin characteristics (such as weight limitations or cold storage capabilities).

Integration with E-Commerce

E-commerce builds on the natural design of an ERP system since it provides electronic communication of basic transactions. Integrated e-commerce functionality is supported in several ways, including Biztalk transactions, reverse auctions, commerce portals, and user portals.

Biztalk Transactions for Sales and Purchasing   The symmetry of sales and purchasing functionality is reflected in Biztalk transactions, as shown in Figure 11.1. For example, an outbound Biztalk sales quote and sales order confirmation can be sent to a customer. Conversely, an inbound Biztalk purchase quote and purchase order confirmation can be received from a vendor. Each inbound transaction can have an optional e-mail notification sent to the internally responsible person.

E-Commerce Sourcing via Reverse Auctions   A reverse auction provides an electronic approach to sourcing a purchase. It includes sending a request for quote to multiple vendors, obtaining vendor responses on a Web site, reviewing the quotes, communicating to vendors whether their quote was accepted or rejected, and creating a purchase order from the quote.

Commerce Portal and User Portal   Supply chain activities often require interaction with remote users and external personnel. The Commerce

	Sales		Purchasing
Outbound	Sales Order Confirmation Shipment Notification Sales Quote Sales Invoice Sales Credit Memo Export Product Catalog	**Inbound**	Purchase Order Confirmation Purchase Receipt Purchase Quote Purchase Invoice Purchase Credit Memo Import Product Catalog
Inbound	Sales Order Request for Sales Quote	**Outbound**	Purchase Order Request for Purchase Quote

Figure 11.1 E-Commerce and Biztalk Transactions for
            Sales and Purchasing

Portal supports creation of Web pages for electronic access to information, such as handling requests for quotes and sending quotes. The User Portal supports information retrieval and task performance by remote users, such as sales tasks to create new quotes, sales orders, and customers.

Integration with Relationship Management

The ability to manage relationships with customers, vendors, and others is fully integrated with standardized functionality for supply chain management. This level of integration contrasts sharply with add-on functionality such as a third-party Customer Relationship Management (CRM) application. Illustrations of integrated functionality include the following.

◆ *Contact Interactions Reflecting Supply Chain Activities.* The system automatically records contact interactions involving sales and purchase documents. For example, an interaction may represent sending a document for a sales quote or invoice, or a purchase quote or order. Each document is treated as an interaction.

◆ *Contact Interactions Reflecting Outgoing Calls, E-Mail, and Cover Letters.* The system automatically records contact interactions involving outgoing communications initiated from within Navision, such as originating a phone call. Outgoing e-mail becomes an attachment to the interaction. Incoming e-mail can also be automatically recorded as a contact interaction and attached to the interaction.

◆ *Contacts.* You can create contacts from existing information about customers and vendors (and vice versa), and automatically create contacts when adding customers and vendors.

◆ *Create Sales Quotes and Orders for an Opportunity.* A sales quote can be defined for an opportunity (where the opportunity represents a potential sale to a contact) and converted to a sales order.

◆ *Contacts and Commerce Portals.* Business with a contact can be conducted through a commerce portal.

Other relationship management capabilities go beyond these integration features. As part of generating and qualifying leads, for example, you can create a campaign, assign a subset of contacts to the campaign, define a template for sending information (such as mailings or e-mail) or making phone calls, and track responses for the campaign. The system automatically records the sent information and responses as contact interactions. Contact interactions can be manually added, and contacts can include banks, accountants, lawyers, travel agencies, government authorities, press, and others. The system supports the identification and tracking of opportunities within user-defined sales cycles, and recording the related contact interactions. Contact information can also serve other purposes, such as printing labels or exporting data for external telemarketing.

Integration with Service Management

Service management typically involves maintenance and repair of products either in the field or at internal repair shops. Firms involved in service management may work on products they have sold or products manufactured and sold by others. A typical example involves an equipment manufacturer that also performs installation services, maintenance on installed units, and/or repairs on returned units. Each unit is termed a service item. Integration of service management with other supply chain functionality is illustrated below.

- *Linkage between a Service Item and Shipped Product.* The shipment transaction automatically creates a service item for each item shipped to a customer, with information about the serial number (if applicable), warranty period, and ship-to location. Service items can also be manually added, which is especially important when working on products not recorded as shipped.

- *Material and Resource Requirements for a Service Order.* A service order can be created with one or more line items identifying the service items to be repaired. Material and resource requirements can be specified for repairing individual line items or for the entire service order. The product's original assembly list can be used to identify needed materials, and the system retains the latest configuration of the repaired unit. Loaners can be sent and received.

Other service management capabilities go beyond these integration features. For example, resource requirements can be identified by skill level and location, which is especially helpful in scheduling field service personnel using the dispatch board capabilities. The system supports service quotes (which can be converted to service orders) and service contracts, troubleshooting diagnostic capabilities, and the identification of faults, symptoms, and resolution related to a service item.

Integration with Accounting Applications

The integrated accounting applications include payables, receivables, general ledger, and fixed assets. Integration of these accounting applications with other supply chain functionality is illustrated below.

Payables   The purchase order receipt transaction can also be used to enter the vendor invoice information. It may have accompanied the incoming material, or the receipt itself represents the invoice. The system handles vendor returns and the associated credit memo information, and customer returns can even spawn vendor returns. Actual costing methods are based on posting the vendor invoice.

Receivables   The sales order shipment transaction can also generate a sales invoice, typically because the invoice must accompany the shipment. The system handles customer returns and the associated credit memo information. The pricing and discount information for sales orders also applies to manually entered invoices and credit memos.

General Ledger   The system provides an audit trail to every supply chain activity that impacts the general ledger. It also supports analysis by analytic dimensions related to items, customers, vendors, and other entities.

Fixed Assets   The fixed assets application is integrated with purchase order and sales order processing. A fixed asset purchase can represent the acquisition or maintenance of a fixed asset, where the line item indicates the fixed asset identifier. Additional information must be indicated on the purchase order line item for an acquisition, and the receipt transaction updates information in the fixed assets application. A fixed asset can also be sold, where the sale order line indicates the identifier for a fixed asset and the sales price, and the shipment transaction updates information in the fixed assets application.

Integration with Business Analytics   Integrated functionality with business analytics has several implications. It simplifies the steps involved in defining and populating information in the data warehouse (especially information related to analytic dimensions), so that minimal time and technical expertise are required for implementation. It provides out-of-the-box functionality for supporting standardized and *ad hoc* analyses. It also supports customization to meet the unique requirements for decision support.

Concluding Remarks

When reviewing or learning any ERP software package, it is important to understand its underlying design philosophies and how it is targeted toward different manufacturing and distribution environments. It is easy to get bogged down in the details. Some of the key design factors that differentiate Microsoft Navision have been summarized here. These design factors influence how the system fits together to run a business, especially the key business processes for managing supply chain activities in manufacturing and distribution.

Appendix

Navision Terminology and Synonyms

System usage is shaped by several design factors. One of these factors is the terminology for window titles, field labels and functions that describe system usage. This book's explanations used the Microsoft Navision terminology as much as possible, but sometimes employed generally accepted synonyms or alternative phrasing to clarify understanding. Several Navision terms require greater clarification, as explained below.

Posting A posting function must be performed before an inventory-related transaction updates the inventory value and/or inventory balance. Illustrations of inventory-related transactions include purchase order receipts, sales order shipments, production order output, and inventory adjustments. The concept of posting allows multiple transactions to be entered and reviewed prior to updating the database. For example, the posting concept allows multiple inventory adjustments to be prepared, and then a single user-initiated function (the posting function) updates the database. The posting function can be performed for a single transaction or a set of transactions and represents a mass-update approach for a set of transactions. As a mass-update approach, the posting function provides immediate on-line notification of errors (such as lot numbering requirements on a receipt transaction) within the set of transactions. Errors can then be corrected before performing the posting function again.

Registering The registering function must be performed before an inventory movement transaction (that does not affect inventory value) updates the database. The key difference with the posting function is that it does not affect inventory value. The registering function applies to warehouse documents used to move material, such as putting away material after posting its receipt, or picking material to a staging area prior to posting its shipment.

Journal A journal typically pertains to general ledger transactions, and a set of inventory transactions that impact inventory value are also termed a journal. Each line item in a journal represents one inventory transaction, and line items can be prepared and modified prior to posting. Journals are used for different types of inventory transactions as shown below.

Journal Name	Type of Transaction
Item Journal	Inventory adjustments
Reclassification Journal	Inventory movements
Physical Inventory Journal	Inventory adjustments related to a physical inventory or a cycle count
Revaluation Journal	Change value of inventory
Consumption Journal	Issue component inventory to production orders
Output Journal	Receive output from production orders into inventory. It is also used to charge work center time against production order routings, thereby impacting WIP inventory value.
BOM Journal	Receive completed kit items into inventory.
Job Journal	Issue inventory to a job. It is also used to report resource time expended on a job.

As noted in the above list, a journal is also used for other types of transactions. This includes the Output Journal for reporting work center time against a production order routing, and the Job Journal for reporting resource time expended on a job. Another journal (the Resource Journal) is used for reporting usage of resource time.

Ledger Entries Several sets of ledger entries represent the inventory transaction audit trail for an item. This audit trail consists of *item ledger entries* and *physical inventory ledger entries*, and the transaction type is termed *ledger entry type*. An item's inventory transaction audit trail also consists of lot and/or serial numbers (based on the item tracking policies) that are identified as *item tracking entries*.

The financial equivalents for an inventory transaction audit trail are termed *item value entries*. An item's value entries identify and segment the financial impact for each inventory-related transaction, such as segmenting a purchase order receipt into direct and indirect costs. With standard costing, item-related value entries also identify variances and changes to standard cost that revalue existing inventory.

There are other sets of ledger entries. *Customer ledger entries* identify the posted shipments and invoices related to a customer; *vendor ledger entries* do the same for a vendor.

Navigation   The Navigation feature allows you to identify the source transaction that created a posted transaction, such as the sales order shipment that created a posted invoice. It also highlights related information, such as item ledger entries and customer ledger entries.

List of Terms and Synonyms   The following list provides the Navision terms and synonyms.

Term	Synonyms
Assembly List	Components of a kit item
Blocked	Hold status
BOM Item	Kit item
BOM Journal	Report completions of a kit item
BOM Line	Component in a bill
BOM Number	Master bill identifier
Break-Bulk	Unpack and repack one UM into another
Capacity Cost	Direct costs for a work center
Capacity Overhead Costs	Indirect costs for a work center
Component Forecast	Independent demand
Cross-Dock Opportunity	Shortage List
Cross-References	Customer item, vendor item, catalog item
Customer ledger entries	Posted invoices, credit memos
Direct Cost	Purchase cost
Flushing Method	Usage policy (manual, back-flush, forward-flush)
Fixed Bin	Authorized bin for an item and location
Invoice discount	Discount (surcharge) related to total order value
Item Journal	Inventory adjustments
Item Ledger Entries	Inventory transaction audit trail
Item Reclassification Journal	Inventory movements
Item Tracking Entries	Transaction history for lot- and serial-traced item
Item Tracking Policy	Lot- and serial-control policies
Item Value Entries	General ledger transaction audit trail
Ledger Entry Type	Transaction type
Location Code	Site, warehouse, stockroom, plant
Manufacturing Overhead Costs	Item-related overhead
MRP Items	Item without independent demand
MPS Item	Item with independent demand
Navigate	Drill-down to source transaction
Order Tracking Data	Pegging to source of demand and supply

Term	Synonyms
Physical Inventory Journal	Record physical inventories and cycle counts
Production Family Item	Identifier for a group of co-products
Production Forecast	Set of forecasted demands consisting of sales forecasts, component forecasts or both
Production Order	Manufacturing order, work order
• Multiline Production Order	Production order with extra line(s) for make-to-order component(s), or generated from a multiline sales order
• Project Order	Production order generated from a multiline sales order
Production Order Components	Order-dependent bill
Production Order Routing	Order-dependent routing
Refresh Production Order	Create order-dependent bill and routing; create line items on a production order
Reordering Policy • Fixed Reorder Quantity • Maximum • Lot-for-Lot • Order • Blank	Replenishment method • Time-phased order point • Time-phased min/max • Period lot size • Order-driven • Manual
Replenishment System	Make/buy/transfer code
Revaluation Journal	Changes to an item's inventory value
Routing Number	Master routing identifier
Sales Forecast	Independent demand
Stockkeeping Unit (SKU)	Authorized location and/or variant code for an item
Transaction Audit Trail	Item ledger entries; item tracking entries, physical inventory ledger entries
Transfer Order	Interplant transfer order
TrendScape	Matrix view of summarized data by time period
Vendor Ledger Entries	Posted invoices, credit memos
Version Number	Version of a master bill; version of a master routing
Warehouse	Location, site, stockroom, plant

Index

LaVergne, TN USA
03 May 2010
181330LV00004B/47/P